on WINE

A MASTER SOMMELIER
AND MASTER OF WINE TELLS ALL

on WINE

A MASTER SOMMELIER
AND MASTER OF WINE TELLS ALL

DOUG FROST

foreword by ROBERT MONDAVI

RIZZOLI
NEW YORK

First published in the United States of America in 2001 by
RIZZOLI INTERNATIONAL PUBLICATIONS, INC.
300 Park Avenue South
New York, NY 10010

ISBN: 0-8478-2335-0
LC: 2001 08 6044

Distributed by St. Martin's Press

Manufactured in Hong Kong, PRC

PHOTO & ILLUSTRATION CREDITS

To Brenda, for her tolerance and guidance through our life together. And to Hannah and Allegra for their wonderful love and patience with Dad's "wine thing."

ACKNOWLEDGMENTS

Thanks to my colleagues, mentors (unknown, inadvertent, and otherwise), and companions on the wine trail: David Adelsheim, Gerald Asher, Bob Bath, Wayne Belding, Dan Berger, Joel Butler, Stephen Carey, Jim Clendenen, Clive Coates, Mike Corso, Fred Dame, Steve Doerner, Charlie Faulk, Bob Foster, Andy Frankel, Tim Gaiser, John Gay, Evan Goldstein, Joshua Greene, Tim Hanni, Mark Huebner, Andrea Immer, Brian Julyan, Dennis Kaniger, Peter Koff, Mendel Kohn, Fran Kysela, David Lake, John Larchet, Leonardo LoCascio, Robert Mondavi, Robert Noecker, Steve Olson, Jorge Ordonez, Robert Parker, Stuart Piggott, John Skupny, Terry Thiese, Madeline Triffon, Michael Weiss, Joshua Wesson, Rudi Wiest, Chad Zimmerman, and Kevin Zraly, and all the others who have taught me so much. Please keep teaching.

I am tremendously indebted to my editor, Elizabeth Viscott Sullivan, who fought for several years to find a home for this book.

My biggest thanks and sincere appreciation go to my friends and family who chose not to ridicule me for being such a wine dweeb, at least to my face.

FOREWORD *8*

INTRODUCTION *10*

CONTENTS

F O R E W O R D

Great advances are occurring in winemaking and grapegrowing throughout the world. Wines are being made in a more international style, which emphasizes the creation of youthful-tasting wine regardless of whether the wines are made in the New World or Old World. Some critics contrast international style with *terroir*, or site specificity, but I believe that the two concepts are harmonious. My experience around the world has shown me that wines can typify a place, yet can also be made more elegantly and full of character.

In this millennium, winemakers will yield an even greater quality of wine than ever before from grapes that are being grown more naturally and have better clonal selection, and from using a larger number of distinct grape varieties from all over the world. Wines will be made more gently, using gravity flow operations and a total lack of filtration for fine wines. This may appear to be a minor change, but it will make a significant difference on the palate.

While there is an unstoppable trend today towards global entities at the producer, importer, distributor, and retail levels, there will always be an important role for the winemaker whose focus is on quality and a passion for excellence.

As a Master of Wine and Master Sommelier, Doug Frost shares in this vision. His knowledge and experience are a great asset to the world of wine; I'm sure you'll enjoy and learn a great deal from his terrific book.

—Robert Mondavi, Napa Valley, California

I N T R O D U C T I O N

During the 1970s and '80s wine sales in America were on the decline. The usual explanation was that people were drinking less but better; while wine sales were down by volume, the dollars being spent increased nearly every year since 1970.

In the late 1990s, wine sales increased by both measures. Yet today, not quite 30 percent of adult Americans drink wine on a monthly basis. Why aren't they attracted to wine's flavors as we wine lovers are?

Me, I'm a flavor craver. I'm a hedonist. I want to taste everything that I can, as often as I can and, sometimes, as much as I can. It's the flavor that I crave, although the alcohol in wine is a nice bonus.

Those of us who are fascinated by flavors often wax esoteric about the whole thing. To us, of course, we're just getting jiggy. But for others who may have known the misfortune of sitting in a room full of wine-ophiles, each pontificating on the pleasures of this week's hot wine, it's hard to remember that wine is only a bottle of flavors.

I'll admit that we wine lovers are often insufferable. If someone tells us about a wine they like, we'll tell them about a wine that's better. Or worse, we'll tell them that the wine or winery they like used to be much better. In our passion for wine we forget that wine is. . . just a drink. Wine is grape juice with alcohol. It has flavors some find enjoyable. Reading books such as this one and talking to other wine drinkers may help you to know some of those flavors. Everything else is just details.

Wine is too often used as a bludgeon by those who know to beat up on those who don't. Every wannabe wine expert, pretending mastery in the subject, has gaping areas of ignorance. So, if someone tries to get smug about the latest Bryant Family or Harlan wine, smirk back and talk about the nice twelve-dollar Spanish wine you just found. Then change the subject and move to a different part of the room.

WINE SMART

"He really knows his wines," is an oft-heard remark about wine lovers, and it makes me twitch. Though there is no one on the planet who knows all "his" wines, I grudgingly admit that there is some truth in the phrase. None of us needs to, or is likely to, know all the wines. If people want to be conversant in wine, they need to know only about those wines they like or might like.

While wine seems to be gaining ground in American life, I worry that wine's complexity intimidates most people. A lot of twenty-somethings have chosen to put wine aside in favor of neon-colored cocktails. Some of those cocktails have pretty interesting histories, but not like wine. These histories help explain some of wine's flavors, as does geography. And understanding where beverages come from adds to the pleasure.

FEAR OF WINE

But, because wine is so multifaceted and multitudinous, it can be overwhelming. The anxiety that accompanies being handed the wine list in a restaurant is about choosing *the wrong wine*, whatever that may be. There is no wrong wine, unless it's wine that doesn't taste good. If that's the case, send it back.

Just bear in mind that other tasters might not agree that a particular wine is bad and they're not necessarily wrong. There are millions of kinds of wines because there are millions of people with their own ideas of what good flavor is. There is no hierarchy in wine: it is not true that one wine is best and another wine is second best. Instead, the question is, best according to whom?

WINE, OUT OF THE BOX

I'm not saying that a box wine is the same as Lafite—it's not. That's the point. One wine may not be better than another, but it's the difference between them that's important. No matter how hard some winemakers may try to create the wine that the *Wine Advocate* or *Wine Spectator* gave one hundred points to last year, they can't. Like fingerprints, no two wines are alike.

That is wine's best asset and biggest problem. It lacks predictability—from vintage to vintage, from region to region, and from taste to taste. Marketers hate that. Lots of consumers hate that too and drink Budweiser instead. It's a personal choice but that unpredictable flavor—whether in food, people, or life—is my favorite part of our existence.

HOW TO USE THIS BOOK

Wine's unpredictability is partly due to our lack of understanding. Although wine is too much of a living thing to be entirely predictable, knowing about grapes, regions, and winegrowing and making can alleviate its mysteriousness. The first chapter explains how we got to where we are today, wine-wise, and how wine is made. Chapter Two presents the basic elements of wine flavor and taste, and defines the different wine styles. The third chapter covers the ninety most important grapes and describes how wines made from them will taste.

Chapters Four and Five describe the traditions of each wine-producing region, because tradition, like history, helps predict how a wine will taste and age. Chapter Four focuses upon the New World and Chapter Five, the Old World. Pairing food and wine is the subject of Chapter Six.

Finally, for label worshippers, the appendices include the all-important "my favorite wines" list. Just try to remember that I have an iced latte every afternoon and I don't expect you to do that, so I'm not sure you should assume that these will become your favorite wines too. Hopefully, you'll just discover some new favorites. A helpful glossary and indispensable bibliography are also included in the appendices.

Most important, having a lot of wine information doesn't mean a thing if you don't taste. So taste. Taste everything you can, in wine and in life.

—Doug Frost

1

Nature's Invention

a short history of wine

Most historians think beer was the first alcoholic beverage produced by man. They're right, of course, because nature doesn't need man to produce wine. Have you ever seen birds eat ripe grapes? They can eat enough to get drunk. Waiting for the grapes to ripen is the only work that is required.

Early man had only to pick grapes and leave them in a pot for a few days to create wine. Perhaps an ill-fitting lid was placed on it and, as the grape juice was attacked by the local yeasts and fermentation began spontaneously, carbon dioxide was released. The lid began to move, even to jump.

Aristotle called alcohol "spirits," because he believed drinking it put spirits in one's head. Early man surely agreed. After the pot stopped making noises, the bravest among them must have drunk some and, for a time, been transformed. In 10,000 B.C., this was probably a great thing. Even today, it can be.

Commercial wine production provided early civilizations with profitable exports; this is partly because those regions that first practiced large-scale trade happened to be wine producers. Also, wine was the most safely consumed and stable beverage for much of human history; therefore, it was highly sought-after by non-wine-producing communities.

Wine was a staple for the European peasantry as well as the landed class. Though vineyards came and went with the economy and fashion, wine remained an important part of the diet of those in wine-producing regions and those with money living in non-wine-producing regions. The preferred wine was either cheap or strong, or both. The two goals were usually in opposition because strong and stable wines from ripe grapes were most often rare.

ABOVE: Sorting grapes in Portugal. OPPOSITE: The process of winemaking has remained essentially unchanged for hundreds, if not thousands, of years.

Throughout most of wine's history, wine has been as ripe as luck would allow. The best wines were those from warm places—with high sugars and alcohol, they had a hope of aging as long as the next harvest. A few lighter-styled wines, such as Champagne, were favored by the wealthy. But in general, light wine—especially light, white wine—is a twentieth-century phenomenon. It is the result of pristine grapes from well-tended vineyards, vinifications in cool— even cold—conditions, and jacketed stainless-steel fermenters.

The modern era of winemaking could be summed up by a phrase from one of its architects, Emile Peynaud, who noted that "the best way to grow old gracefully, is to stay young as long as possible." Those who say that the nineteenth century was the Golden Age of wine are dead wrong. With more great wines from more places in the world than ever before, *this* is the Golden Age.

THE STUFF OF WINE

What's in wine? Mostly water, a little alcohol (8 to 20 percent by volume), and a few different acids, including tartaric with a little citric and succinic. The characteristics that make wine

interesting are the trace elements remaining. When all the liquid is removed from a wine, the remainder is called the dry extract. European producers sometimes brag about the amount of dry extract in their wines: 28 grams of dry extract is pretty good, 33 grams connotes a massive wine.

But more extract is not necessarily a better wine, no matter what experts say. Balance, elegance, finesse, and breed are all subjective words that describe why some wines are more interesting than others, but these attributes can't be measured by machines.

HOW WINES ARE BUILT

Each bottle of wine has structure which enables the wine to live for more than a week, and that structure varies with the region and style of the wine. In general, white wines are built of fruitiness and acidity, that tart lemon-lime note at the end of a crisp wine. Even more generally, red wines can be built of fruitiness and acidity, fruitiness and tannin, or all three. Tannin is a kind of acidity that gives a dusty astringency and a slight bitterness to a taste. Tea and coffee have tannin, walnuts have tannin; if you've ever left a tea bag to steep for too long, you've experienced the metallic astringency that is tannin.

LEFT: Tea and walnuts have plenty of tannin. RIGHT: Rioja, like Beaujolais, has little tannin and plenty of acidity, while Zinfandel (right) has little acidity and lots of tannin.

Consider two examples: French Beaujolais most often has very little tannin, but plenty of acidity; Zinfandel usually has lots of tannin but very little acidity. Each is fine, and each gives a different sensation.

Up until the 1970s it was thought that red wine should have fairly high levels of both tannin and acidity to be properly structured for aging. That idea is now on yesterday's scrap heap. This understanding reflects a twentieth-century revolution in winemaking that is the driving force in improving wines worldwide.

As much as winemaking has improved, the interesting truth is that it is little different now than it was for early man. Grapes are picked, crushed, and allowed to ferment. Then they are placed in a container prior to drinking. The only difference between winemaking then and now is that we can make choices about the temperature at which this happens, how much air gets to the juice or wine, what size and kind of containers are used, and how long the wine is stored in them.

All our technology is spent in understanding what happens so that we know *when* to do something. But the steps are essentially the same, since wine is nature's, not man's, invention.

BARRELS OF FUN

Through the late twentieth century, American winemakers placed enormous importance upon the barrels they used. And, in the 1970s, many California winemakers were strangely embarrassed by their traditional use of American oak barrels, as French barrels were perceived to be superior.

This perception is at odds with history. Prior to the late twentieth century, most oaks in use were Baltic or Slavic in origin; Bordeaux utilized American oak between the World Wars. But European and American oak barrels were usually made by different methods. Why?

The two continents have different species of oak, but the processes used to make each were more important. Historically, European oak was dried outdoors for three or more years, in order to soften the impact of the oak. American oak was typically dried in a kiln and aged for no more than six months. European barrels were lightly toasted on the inside over oak chips.

LEFT AND RIGHT: These nearly hundred-year-old Portuguese oak trees are stripped for sheets of bark to be cut into corks. They'll soon grow a new layer of bark.

The grapes are brought into the winery.

The grape stems have been removed to lower the tannin in the wine.

FOLLOW THE STEPS OF WINEMAKING

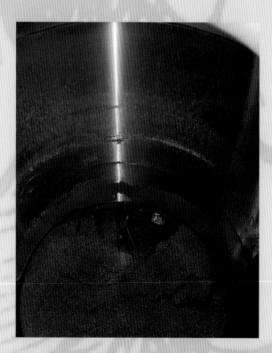

Yeast has been added to begin the fermentation, though some winemakers prefer not to add yeast but to allow the natural yeasts to cause the fermentation.

The wine may be allowed to sit for another two to three weeks, while more color, flavors, and aromas are leached from the skins. Then the wine is racked, or pumped, out of the tank and into barrels.

Depending upon the winemaker and the intended style, grapes may be both destemmed and crushed, destemmed but not crushed, crushed but not destemmed, or dumped whole into the fermenter, stems and all.

These grapes are being crushed in a gentle bladder press.

AT STONE HILL WINERY IN MISSOURI

The pomace (the leftover skins and yeast) is removed from the fermenter and may be used as fertilizer in the vineyards.

The wines have been placed into American oak barrels. They are aged in barrels for a year or more. The kind, size, maker, and wood origin of the barrel can profoundly alter the wine.

American barrels were visibly burnt on the inside, perhaps to sterilize the containers, because up until the end of the nineteenth century, barrels were widely used for transportation of virtually all goods.

Those differences have become far less pronounced today. American oak barrels are being made in classic European methods now and are less intense. At the same time French barrel-makers, under pressure to increase production, have shortened the aging time for their staves.

The character that a younger oak barrel imparts to wine is mostly aromatic and textural; it can make a wine creamy, thick, astringent, even bitter, but it's always spice-laden. Aromas of black pepper, ginger, allspice, nutmeg, clove, and vanilla are common; young American oak will often add an herbal note, such as a vanilla bean or even dill or coconut.

Today, alternate barrel sources, such as Hungary and Oregon, are gaining ground and the biases for French oak are softening.

VITICULTURE—HOMEGROWN IS BEST

Row orientation and windbreaks can influence the intensity of sun, wind, and rain in the vineyard.

The winegrowing process also hasn't changed over the years. And today, there are those who believe that the ancient, even mystic, methods of viticulture hold the best new ideas. In the pre-modern world, tension always existed between ripeness and cheapness. Many mid-twentieth-century vintners believed they could achieve huge quantities, as well as ripeness, not believing that it would deter quality. It did.

The late twentieth century saw the pendulum swing back to smaller quantities, sometimes to absurd extremes. Today, most knowledgeable viticulturalists recognize that

each plant, each region, and each grape has a balanced point, at which the plant is healthy and the resulting wine is as good as it can be from that site.

SITE SPECIFIC

Understanding the impact of site is the most important task of every winegrower. The possible influences are nearly endless. Macroclimate and mesoclimate are fancy words for the larger grape-growing region that explain the temperature and moisture variance during and after the growing cycles. Severe night and day temperature swings tend to create very different flavors than more consistent cycles.

The term *microclimate* describes the most local influences and includes topographical features such as hills, mountains, lakes, oceans, and forests. Bodies of water tend to moderate temperature swings, forests can hold moisture, and mountains may block or cause wind or rain.

Soil characteristics have a profound but much-argued impact on the flora and fauna of the vineyard, from the yeasts present to the nutrients in and flavor from the grapes. The most impotant element is drainage; rarely do vines in wet soils produce good wine. But the pH, nutrient content or lack thereof, subsoil textures, and even the cation exchange capacity can all change the quality of the wine.

The angle, aspect, and elevation of the vineyard impacts the temperature cycles, frost problems, and the sun exposure on differing parts of the plant, changing the ripening cycle of the grapes.

There are several other local topographical features to consider. For example, eucalyptus trees in Australia and northern California can, when grown near vineyards, add a minty element to the wine. Windbreaks are imperative in places such as Tasmania. In the dessert-wine regions of Bordeaux, fog produced by nearby rivers creates botrytis, the noble rot that sweetens wines.

Proximity to particular habitats can impact the kinds of pests and diseases with which wine growers must contend. Today, Pierce's Disease is destroying parts of California's vineyards because there are friendly places for the sharpshooters (the insects that spread the disease) to live. Birds pose a constant threat to grapes in places as far-flung as New Zealand and Oregon.

Taken together, these site characteristics form what the French (and all others now) call *terroir*. The hand of man is part of the concept of *terroir*. How?

Trellising, training, trimming, spraying, pruning and preparing of the vines, spacing of those vines, and especially the selection of grapes, clones, and rootstocks used are methods of improving the wines or changing yields—and are constantly changing.

Yields have a profound impact on quality. It's as though every vine has a certain amount of flavor to give; flavor can be diluted among twenty bunches or concentrated among five.

Working the soil, additions such as fertilizers, and organic and bio-dynamic agriculture methods (see Glossary) all require myriad decisions with even more effects on the wine, intended and otherwise.

Irrigation is illegal throughout most of France, but French vineyards are usually well supplied from annual rainfall. For those in drier climates, the timing of irrigation can have an amazing impact.

Availability of labor, supplies, and markets impact the pricing of a wine and, for most people, the price is the most important aspect of a wine. Certain areas allow machine harvesting, though some believe that method lessens quality. However, machine harvesting can lower prices and improve the condition of fruit in some hot areas, thus allowing areas without available labor to have alternatives.

Though our understanding of the vine's needs and wine's cycles improves with each vintage, we have only one harvest each year to understand a vineyard. Give us another thousand and we should have this thing down cold.

PREVIOUS PAGE: The precipitous Mosel Valley is a study in the importance of aspect towards the sun and of solar reflection from the river. ABOVE: Château d'Yquem, the greatest estate in Sauternes, a region dependent upon fog and humidity for the character of its sweet wines.

2

Styles, Tastes, and Aromas

Unfortunately, the popular concepts of aroma and taste are currently far off-kilter. The media have promoted the concept of super-tasters, people with unusually keen senses of taste. It's not true. We all have more or less the same equipment.

For one, most writers speak of four flavors: sweet, sour, salt, and bitter. That concept is badly outdated in that it ignores at least one other flavor, umami (this is discussed in greater detail in Chapter 6). These flavors act in concert and sometimes cancel each other out; discussing one flavor by itself ignores reality.

Second, we don't taste much anyway—we smell what's in our mouths. When we say that something tastes good, we say this because the food or drink is not bitter and because it smells and tastes like something familiar to us.

An aroma's interest, disinterest, or repugnance is based upon familiarity. If a wine smells like grandma's cooking, our favorite garden, or fresh fruit, we usually like it. If it smells odd or even has smells that we do not expect in a glass of wine, most of us will reject it. As we grow older, we try new foods and beverages and consequently become familiar with more flavors. Familiarity, when we were young, was a survival skill—eating what your parents taught you to eat was smart behavior. Today we call those familiar flavors "comfort foods." Smells may be based entirely upon experience and familiarity. The experience is both learned and innate.

Combine taste, smells, textures, other physio-chemical reactions and responses to the familiar and not-familiar, and you have flavor. In order to communicate with each other about style, we must first talk about flavor.

Several examples of rosés.

HOW TO SPEAK WINE

Even though flavor is composed of many components, speaking of them communicates nothing, because we taste by familiarity. Using descriptors from the real world—fruits, vegetables, plants, trees, earth—anything real that we can commonly recall makes more sense.

In America we try to communicate wine by giving it a number, such as 94 points, but this says nothing about the flavor. In Europe, they speak not of numbers, and often not of varieties, but of place. The goodness or lack thereof has been judged by the wine's typicity—its similarity to other wines from that place.

What is most exciting to me about wine is that it can, without question, reflect the place it's grown so completely that it has flavors and aromas that can only come from that place and no other. This may sometimes change my assessment of the wines of a place.

For instance, I used to think that many Pinot Noirs from Oregon's Red Hills area were not to my liking because the producers were simply not among the best. Despite the fact that producers such as Erath and Rex Hill make markedly

28

better wines than they did twenty years ago (who doesn't?), my mind-set changed completely when I realized that the allspice aromas and mineral-like flavors I negatively associated with those wineries were in fact characteristics of the place. Suddenly, the wines were fascinating. This was an aroma I couldn't get anywhere else in my Pinot Noir, therefore it was good.

Why would anyone be interested in trying a bottle of earthy Burgundy, especially when it's described as having a barnyard smell? Who would order a bottle of Sancerre or Pouilly-Fumé, when its smell is described as cat's pee on a gooseberry bush with a dirty-socks note?

It's not simply that we're throwing absurdly foul descriptors on an otherwise pleasant drink. Those aromas are there, alongside other more typically appetizing ones.

EXPECTATIONS BEFORE EXPECTORATIONS

As a sommelier, I saw that tasters liked best those wines that confirmed their expectations of the wines. I also saw that I could greatly influence people's perception of the quality of a wine by pointing out what was most pleasant about the wine just before they drank it.

This occurs even when the wine would not normally be to their liking. Plenty of people dislike tannic, red wine. But if I describe the dusty texture and the spicy aromas associated with these sorts of wines, allowing people to find the smells before they actually taste it, their reactions change. Thus, the so-called educated palate may simply have been shown some of these flavors, resulting in different expectations from someone who has never been told that these flavors are legitimate and, perhaps, even pleasant.

YOUR TASTE OR MINE?

What is most important to remember is that this in no way means that people should like the wine. It simply means that they now have a *chance* to like the wine. You don't tell me I'm wrong to like apple juice and I'm not saying you shouldn't drink sweetened tea. So why do people snigger at White Zinfandel drinkers? Could it be that they have only recently "graduated" to the more expensive beverages?

WHEN TALKING ABOUT WINE. . . STYLE IS EVERYTHING

Just ask my teenage daughter. She tolerates my inept sense of style but, for her, it's a big deal. I try to have a more sanguine attitude, including my prejudices toward and against certain styles of wine.

All wine drinkers, including wine writers, have styles of wine they prefer. When I am asked the inevitable question about my "favorite wine," I cringe and recite some trite answer about liking all kinds of wines. But that shabby lie is easily exposed by a trip to my cellar. There certain labels, regions, and, above all, styles proliferate.

I tend to drink tart white wines; earthy whites and reds; fruity and spicy reds; fat, rich bubblies (when the wife is in the mood); old wines from anywhere; and fortified wines with dessert, if we have guests. If it sounds as though I don't drink a lot of big, rich, oak-laden reds and whites, it's true. I *taste* them a lot, because they're very popular, but I don't often drink them.

My strongest complaint about the current state of wine writing is that most reviewers reward big wines with big reviews. Therefore, readers who aren't as enamored of "massive," "full-throttle wines" with "bucket-loads of hedonistic fruit" and all that pablum, don't get a lot of guidance. Instead, readers want help finding wines similar to the ones they already like—in other words, they need to know the style of the wine.

WHY AREN'T WINES SOLD BY STYLE?

They are. If you visit good retailers or sommeliers, they ask you what you like and suggest wines in a similar style. Many of the wine lists written these days will separate wines into style; sometimes helpfully, sometimes obliquely.

No one intended to obfuscate this issue. It's just that the regions in which wine was first produced didn't use varietal names. They certainly didn't compare their wines to the rest of the world by using style words such as earthy and spicy; they didn't even drink the wines of the rest of the world.

The European tradition of naming the wine after the region in which it's grown is a historical necessity. The grapes we know today by one name had numerous nicknames. For instance, Cabernet Franc has been grown throughout France since antiquity and found its way into northern Italy about two centuries ago. During the last hundred years or so it has been known by names such as Breton, Carmenet, Bouchet, Gros Bouchet, Grosse Vidure, Veron, Bouchy, Noir-Dur, Méssange Rouge, Trouchet Noir, Bordo, and—in Italy—Cabernet Frank.

Today, regardless of where the grape is grown, there is a common expectation of style. That is, I expect a Cabernet Franc good enough to be bottled and sold on the world market to be a fairly rich, red wine, with sweet cherry flavors and an herbal note that can vary from lightly spicy to intensely green pepperish. It may have oak spices or it may not be aged in oak, but either way it usually has some earthiness.

UNDERSTANDING STYLE

The use of varietal names such as Cabernet Franc is a phenomenon of the 1960s but, like yoga, has stuck around. Because the New World is too new to have a tradition of certain grapes from certain places, these grape names have been used to communicate flavors. It has served us well so far. . . or has it? Chardonnay can be made in a variety of styles; it can be fruity, even sweet, lightly scented by oak, or with two-by-fours fairly floating in the glass. It can be crisp and tart, or buttery enough to dunk lobster in it. And Chardonnay is by no means the most extreme example. Riesling is made from pancake-syrup sweet to face-suckingly dry. Merlot can vary from thin and weedy (think wet weeds) to rich and chocolatey.

The numerical method of wine reviewing is supposed to ferret out the thin from the rich. But is an 89-point Merlot better than an 87-Cabernet or a 91-point Syrah? Indeed the system suggests a specificity of wine evaluation that is completely ludicrous. Wine circles love to recount tales of well-known magazines unknowingly scoring the same wine with widely variant scores, simply because the labels were different.

This is not to suggest duplicity, but rather that wines change. This is why wine is much more fascinating than milk. Milk changes, but only in one direction. Wine can go anywhere: downhill, uphill, or sideways, sometimes all at once.

The legitimate frustration for a wine buyer lies in not knowing how the wine will taste. In the Grapes chapter that follows, the majority of the grapes listed are created in a somewhat uniform style and so the grape name is going to be the key.

But the world's most widely planted grapes can be found in many styles. Indeed, this is because they are planted in so many places. The grape plus the region generally equals the style. The following chapters describe grape flavors, and then the tendencies of certain regions to produce those grapes in a particular style.

There was a time when the only great wines were those that aged. That time is long past, though you wouldn't know it from wine reviewers who champion only the agers. Rather than insist that my taste is something more objective, I'll describe those grapes and regions which, for me, exemplify certain styles.

The style categories include light and aromatic white wines and white wines that are marked by time in oak barrels. In reds we can speak of lighter and softer reds, earthier reds, and intense reds. The other key styles are sparkling wine, fortified wine, and/or dessert wine.

Aromatic white-wine varieties usually aren't barrel-aged because utilizing oak fermentation or storage would interfere with the aromas. The aroma is the winemaker's motivation for focusing upon these grapes. These include Riesling, Gewürztraminer, Pinot Gris, Pinot Blanc, Grüner Veltliner, Muscat, Cortese, Viognier, Sylvaner, Müller-Thurgau, Arneis, Trebbiano, Albariño, Roussanne, Marsanne, Chenin Blanc, Malvasia, and Garganega. Whites that may be aged in barrels include Sémillon, Sauvignon Blanc, and Chardonnay. These are the sorts of wines that garner the most attention and critical acclaim, but are no more likely to age well than those that are not aged in oak.

The grapes that are usually made into softer, lighter reds include Barbera, Dolcetto, Gamay, Malbec, Pinot Meunier, Cinsaut, Aleatico, and Grignolino. Earthier reds can include Carignan, Grenache (Garnacha Tinta), Pinotage, Sangiovese, Tempranillo, Pinot Noir, Mourvèdre, Aglianico, Gaglioppo, Carmenere, and Malbec. The following grapes are invariably used to produce intense reds: Cabernet Franc, Merlot, Nebbiolo, Cabernet Sauvignon, Syrah, Zinfandel, Petit Verdot, Montepulciano, Sagrantino, Baga, and Tannat.

Grape varieties need not remain in a particular category on this scale but can sometimes be created in styles from soft to intense. Moreover, certain vintages offer more intensity than others. Neither the grape alone nor the region alone can predict the style of the wine. In the Grapes chapter that follows, each grape is described in order to help you predict its style.

3

Grapes

the flavor finder

The following are the most important grapes any wine drinker is likely to experience. Keep in mind that grape varieties are a relatively new phenomenon for wine writers and drinkers. Knowing varietal names is a red herring. It is more helpful to understand that these grapes are merely a means to an end because the vast majority of the great wines of the world are blends. That means that varietal names are only part of the story. I've defined the varieties here by the flavors *usually* found. Because varietal names offer this definition, they've become the method by which wines are marketed in America and elsewhere, but they tell only a fraction of the story.

WHITE-WINE GRAPES

AIRÉN: This is the most widely planted grape in the world. The fun wrinkle is that it is planted in only one place, the vast plain of La Mancha in central Spain, and is used for brandy. However, the plantations there exceed worldwide plantations of any other grape, including Chardonnay.

ALBARIÑO: A lovely floral-scented grape that is still unheralded outside of northwest Spain and northern Portugal. It doesn't age well, but neither does American Chardonnay and that hasn't prevented its storied success. When ripe, Albariño has orange, lemon, and pear flavors; it is not herbaceous but floral and flattering. It is also called Alvarinho in Vinho Verde, Portugal.

ALIGOTÉ: Though a fun little trollop of a grape, it occupies only a small portion of the acreage of Burgundy, as white-wine vineyards are devoted to Chardonnay. It's best when dressed up in its mistress's finery, as when Burgundy producers age Aligoté in brand-new or slightly used Burgundy oak barrels. That's when its tart lemony character is subdued by the toasty oak. It does not age.

ARNEIS: A very attractive and floral grape which tends to be low in acidity and so doesn't age well. For those in love with its honey-lemon-orange-pear flavors, it's a lovely drink in its first few years. It's native to Piedmont, Italy.

BOURBOULENC: The primary white grape of the southern Rhône in France, it comprises the majority of the blend in most white Châteauneuf-du-Pape. It's very lemony and usually characterless, though it can age well.

BROWN MUSCAT (see Muscat of Alexandria, page 39): This is the Muscat that is always encountered as a sweet wine. A favorite base of Australian dessert wines (called stickies). Expect honey and even caramel and tangerine sweetness.

BUAL: see Madeira, Chapter 5, page 114.

CHARDONNAY: It is the most popular varietal bottle of white wine in the world, mostly because it's easy to produce at a reasonable price in many different environments. The flavor of the wine is fairly light, with pear and peach notes, and mineral and stony flavors in certain regions.

Chardonnay's market dominance reflects its willingness to adapt to a winemaker's methods, whether light and crisp, sweet and buttery, or saturated with the burnt toast smells of new oak barrels. The wildly popular style of oak-dominated aromas and flavors is ample evidence that power over elegance is preferred by most wine drinkers.

The style and flavor of Chardonnay can be predicted, to a degree, by its place of origin. Burgundy, where Chardonnay offers its greatest expressions, is rarely as toasty as the wines of the New World. Its intensity varies from lean and stony (as in Chablis, Mâcon, and most Pouilly-Fuissé) to rich and mouth-filling (as with Meursault, Chassagne-Montrachet, and Corton-Charlemagne). Chardonnay from the south of France, often labeled as vin de Pays d'Oc, is an interesting hybrid of the two styles.

The rest of Europe follows a course that is more out of step with the international style of toasty and rich. Italian and Spanish versions are very lean and pear-flavored, the richness of a Gaja or Jean León bottling being the exception. Most try to express not barrels but region. The rest of Eastern Europe would still love to be in on the party; Bulgaria has done a creditable job of providing good value Chardonnay, as has Hungary.

But for now, the style makers are in the New World. California created what South African writer John Platter has called the "wide-bodied" style of Chardonnay, with tail fins of oak. It wasn't long before the canny Aussies brought similar models into the showroom.

Today, the New World style of Chardonnay varies from hedonistically rich and high-alcohol to more elegant and longer-lived wines. And areas in Washington State, Oregon, and New Zealand (cooler places) have begun to produce Chardonnays that are decidedly sturdier and more tart than a typical California Chardonnay. South Africa has created surprising versions of cool climate Chardonnays, too, as has Chile.

But the question begged by all of this shifting fortune and morphing style-making is, will one style of Chardonnay eventually prevail? Will California or French or even Australian Chardonnay become dominant simply because it embodies this preferred style? Chardonnay is in fact the battleground for those who, like me, believe that wines from different places are supposed to taste differently, and any attempt to create a single, international style is bad for wine.

CHENIN BLANC: Considered to be a poor man's Chardonnay in America and South Africa. While there's a lot of Chenin Blanc grown in both countries, none is capable of the character and standing of good Chardonnay. However, when grown on the limestone-clay soils along the middle part of the Loire River in France, the grape takes on a new name (Pineau de la Loire) and new qualities. Whether sweet or dry (or even sparkling), the grape has shocking longevity—thirty years or more in great vintages—and has flavors of honey and honeysuckle, crushed leaves, mulch, and sometimes even cheese rind. But that's good.

CORTESE: The grape of Gavi was one of Italy's first international white-wine success stories. To taste it is to wonder why. Light, lean and, at its best, delicate to the point of invisibility, it was a fifteen-second cause célèbre in the 1970s. Although it is still popular in Italy, it is less so in the rest of the world but still worthy of attention.

FAVORITA: It is usually dismissed by wine writers, even Italophiles. Light and perhaps inconsequential in even the best examples, it nonetheless has a crisp pear and lemon note that I find perfect for a warm day. I am not alone. The Favorita producers of Piedmont have a poster and even a book about the grape. So there.

FURMINT: This is the primary grape of Hungary's brilliant dessert wine Tokaji, supported by the grapes Hárslevelü and Muscat.

GARGANEGA: The primary grape of quality Soave, it can arise in dry, sweet, passito (or raisined), and barrel-aged versions. The good examples show apple and pear with stone and leaf in the background, and the passito versions are wonderfully sweet, although they have a note of leafiness.

Chevalier Montrachet, one of the greatest vineyards on the planet, is solely devoted to Chardonnay.

GEWÜRZTRAMINER: It has the musky, floral aromas typical of Muscat varieties and, while the grape's name is frequently translated as "spicy Traminer," it is better to think of it as a more

aromatic version of grapes such as Riesling, Pinot Gris, Pinot Blanc and, okay, Traminer. It can be full-bodied to the point of heaviness and bitterness. Alsace wine producers often show the wine after dessert, even when it is not produced in a sweet style. Rather, the wine is so pungent that it's too overwhelming for most food.

In the New World, Gewürztraminer is often a bit bitter, overly warm in alcohol and too perfumed to be perfectly pleasurable. But cooler sites such as in New Zealand and Chile are showing excellence.

GRÜNER VELTLINER: This grape has lovely pear and white pepper flavors, and a clean but herbaceous note like mustard seed. The top growers create wines of intensity and texture, with fairly high alcohol but virtually no oak. For me, that is another reason to champion this grape.

LOUREIRO: A blending grape used in some of the more expensive versions of Portugal's cheap carafe wine, Vinho Verde, it can be delightful when allowed to dominate the blend. Think honey, flowers, lemons, and apples.

MACABEO: see Viura, page 44.

MALMSEY (ALSO MALVAZIA OR MALVASIA): see Madeira, Chapter 5, page 114.

MARSANNE: It is the primary white grape of the northern Rhône Valley in France, although a few traditional producers there still include some of the Roussanne grape in their bottlings of St.-Joseph, Crozes-Hermitage, or Hermitage Blanc. Marsanne is grown by a few Californians as well as two Aussie houses; in both places it is frighteningly low in acid and short-lived, but fat in flavor and full of orange and honey.

MAUZAC: Used to make traditional sparkling wine from Limoux in southern France, where it's often blended with a touch of Chardonnay; it offers extremely high value.

MELON: Though it offers mostly crisp and characterless white wine from Muscadet, it can be a satisfying and perfect quencher. It has been mistakenly planted and sold as Pinot Blanc in California, providing proof that the grape has latent tastiness.

MÜLLER-THURGAU: This grape was created in 1882 by crossing Germany's greatest grape, Riesling, with its most prolific grape, Silvaner, in hopes of achieving both quality and quantity. Clearly the latter was the outcome, though it has good moments in Germany's Franken.

MUSCADELLE: It usually shows up as a tiny fraction of the blend that comprises sweet wines in the Bordeaux area. Some Sauternes and Barsac producers swear by that tiny amount.

MUSCAT OF ALEXANDRIA: A Muscat variety (see Brown Muscat, page 34.) widely grown in Spain and Greece. It shows up in some Muscats made in southern France and is widely planted in South Africa as Hanepoot.

MUSCAT BLANC À PETITS GRAINS: More respected than its sibling Muscat of Alexandria, it provides the juice for France's most respected Muscats, such as Muscat de Beaumes-de-Venise, Muscat de Lunel, and Muscat de Frontignan. It's the excellent Muscat used in Greece and Portugal, and is known as *Muscat Canelli* in Italy. The grape shows great stuff in the freshness of a very young Moscato d'Asti, when all the primary aromas of the grape are preserved by the Charmat process (see Glossary) and when the bottle is only a few months old.

OPPOSITE: Grüner Veltliner grapes create crisp and rich wines that are popular with the critics, but can be pricey.
ABOVE: The floral intensity of Muscat makes it a frequent base for dessert wine.

MUSCAT OTTENEL: This is Alsace's Muscat of choice and has been propagated in the New World, though it's a fairly neutral and boring subvariety of Muscat. Ottenel often seems to have the greatest amount of the musky aroma that gives the Muscat family its name, without the fruitiness that makes the others such a joy.

PALOMINO: Sherry's primary grape also has an iteration in South Africa and California, where the grape makes decent brandy. In the Jerez region of Andalucía, Spain, it creates one of the world's greatest fortified wines.

PARELLADA: It is the best grape of Cava—Spain's sparkling wine. It's probably the longest-lived and most structured of the Cava grapes—Parellada, Macabeo, and Xarel-lo. As producers pursue quality, most use higher percentages of Parellada and may indeed add Chardonnay.

PINOT BLANC (PINOT BIANCO): Wines from this grape are not on the official Grand Cru (see Glossary) list in Alsace, France. It's unlikely to produce wines of more than a few years ageability, no matter where it is grown. Pinot Bianco, the Italian version, can be just as tasty—expect pears and apples and a slightly slippery buttery note.

PINOT GRIS (PINOT GRIGIO): This grape creates a wine that is always fat and drinkable, even low in acidity, but can live a surprisingly long time (up to twenty years or so). Apple pie with some ripe pear slices—that's my favorite blind-tasting descriptor when a great Alsace Pinot Gris is in my glass. Even with colder sites in Italy, such as Alto Adige and Oltrepò Pavese, Pinot Grigio can be very generous. It is known as Rülander in Germany. The grape remains both rich and aromatic in the New World, with Oregon and New Zealand showing the most promise.

RIESLANER: This is a high-quality German crossing of Silvaner and Riesling, with a rich, broad flavor that easily makes up for its relative lack of ageability; simply put, it won't age twenty or more years as Riesling can. But, when it tastes this great early on, who cares?

RIESLING: Many wine lovers believe this is the world's greatest white grape. In the cold regions of Germany, the grape has brilliant peach, pear, apple, melon, apricot, and floral notes. It drinks delightfully when young and ages for a shockingly long time.

Riesling's youthful beauty belies its singular longevity: How can a wine that tastes delicious at one or two years of age live for two or more decades? Amongst the world's popular grapes, only Riesling and Syrah seem to show this versatility.

Excellent Riesling is grown in Austria and Alsace (in France), and there are remarkable examples in Australia and New Zealand, although most of these show less finesse than great German Riesling. Finesse, in this case, is due to lower alcohol levels. Germany's Mosel River may produce wines of less than 9 percent alcohol; Austria, Australia, and Alsace will offer wines of nearly 15 percent alcohol but which carry similar fascination. In the rest of the world's vineyards, the wine is entirely pleasant but usually has little of this power and grace.

ROUSSANNE: It's used in small percentages in some bottlings of Hermitage Blanc in the northern Rhône Valley of France and is planted in the south, most famously at Châteauneuf-du-Pape. Though it can often seem to be oxidizing before one's nose, it retains that nutty character as well as its distinctive honeysuckle and orange scents for years.

SAUVIGNON BLANC: A clean, usually refreshing white wine, with styles that range from intensely fruity to intensely herbaceous. The historical models of Pouilly-Fumé and Sancerre (among others) in the Loire Valley in France are wines of earthiness and tart pear, melon, and grapefruit. In Bordeaux the wine is usually blended with Sémillon for both the dry and sweet versions, and can have the toasty, spicy aromas derived from new oak barrels. American versions are sometimes called Fumé-Blanc.

New Zealand has reenergized the Sauvignon Blanc market worldwide and proven that some varieties, seemingly set in their ways, can be created in new styles. Whether you like the pungent intensity of Kiwi Sauvignon or not, it has redefined the possibilities of Sauvignon Blanc.

SCHEUREBE: It is an intensely aromatic vinifera crossing (see Glossary) with apricot flavors and lack of ageability. Still it represents the most successful of the more common crossings—Siegerebe, Huxelrebe, Kerner, Rieslaner, and Ehrenfelser.

SÉMILLON: The grape can arrive in a variety of disguises: it can be tart, bracingly clean, and long-lived in Australia; it can be the rich and longest-lived component of a white Bordeaux blend; and it can stand in for Chardonnay in Aussie blends or in New World oak-dominated versions. The latter fools most tasters—it seems uncannily like Chardonnay, simply because most drinkers assume oak barrel flavors are Chardonnay. Any rich white grape with those notes is easily mistaken for Chardonnay. It also provides the sweet soul of great Sauternes and Barsac.

SERCIAL: see Madeira, Chapter 5, page 114.

SEYVAL BLANC: It is not a vinifera vine but a hybrid, created by crossing a vinifera vine with a native American vine. Such hybrid vines have proven extremely useful in harsh, continental climates. This useful hybrid vine gives a wine good balance with pear and grapefruit flavors.

SILVANER: Usually light and insipid, even in its traditional regions of Alsace and Alto Adige. In Franconia, Germany, though, bottles of Silvaner from a good vintage and a good producer are quite long-lived.

TREBBIANO (UGNI BLANC): It is a grape that appears most successfully as a brandy. Vitually all Cognac and most Armagnac utilize 100 percent of wine from this grape. In Italy, where it's widely planted, most bottlings of the wine are boring.

VERDEJO: This grape is grown primarily in the Rueda region of Spain. There is an almond character to most Verdejo, but it has the weight and character to seem almost Chardonnay-like.

VERDELHO: see Madeira, Chapter 5, page 114.

VERDICCHIO: Due to its past iteration in fish-shaped bottles, this is a much-maligned grape grown in central Italy. But not all wines with the name Verdicchio should be painted with the same fishy brush. Delicious versions that are light-bodied with crisp pear and lemon notes exist in standard wine bottles.

VERNACCIA: It is less popular than it once was, but the little white wine from the beautiful town of San Gimignano in Italy is often a very good drink. It is usually quite light but crisp and with a hint of peach. There are other grapes called Vernaccia from other Italian areas that are less frequently exported.

VIDAL BLANC: It is another succesful nonvinifera hybrid with very clean, rich, apricotlike flavors. It is also known as Ravat.

ABOVE: Geyser Peak Viognier from northern California. OPPOSITE: Brunello, one of the best clones of the Sangiovese grape.

VIGNOLES: A successful hybrid with floral, peach, and apricot notes.

VIOGNIER: The quintessential rags-to-riches grape story has been comfortably ensconced in its traveling clothes for a decade and a half. The Pays d'Oc in France has plenty of it planted and California has tried on the suit as well. But in truth, at least as far as California is concerned, Viognier is looking a bit ragged these days. Condrieu in the northern Rhône, and its flagship Château-Grillet, were the last resting places of this fascinating grape in the 1950s, when it was plucked from the grave by a few enterprising and famous French chefs. It was a marvelous match for many seafood dishes and, by the 1970s, Americans decided to give it a go. Initial praise was fulsome and the heady talk went straight to the wine. Bottlings were high in alcohol and often smothered in oak aromas. Though it is still widely planted today, producers admit that the public response has been a bit of a resounding thud. Newer bottlings are crisper and more fruity than oaky and are much improved.

VIURA: The white grape of Rioja delivers higher acidity and lots of floral and pear flavors. As Macabeo in Spanish Cava country, it adds much of the weight and fruitiness of the blend.

WELSCHRIESLING: While the grape is as humble as its varied names—Riesling Italico, Laski Riesling, and Olasz Rizling—it can produce tasty wines, in particular, great dessert wines, laden with the honeyed flavors of botrytis in the warm, wet vineyards of southeast Austria.

RED-WINE GRAPES

AGLIANICO: It makes powerful yet approachable wines from Campania and Basilicata in southern Italy. The greatest expression thus far is in the elevated vineyards on Mount Vulture and in the Taurasi bottlings of Mastroberardino.

ALEATICO: It has amazing aromas when produced in a light, sweet style or, even when made into a fuller-bodied, even fortified, version. Expect strawberry flavors with honey and flowers.

ALICANTE BOUSCHET: It is a vinifera crossing bred from Grenache, among others, in the 1870s, which carries the distinction of being a Teinturier, or grape with pigmented juice. It is unusual, as most grapes have clear juice, allowing for red grapes to produce rosé wines. Alicante is always clumsy but is exaggeratedly rich and spicy, with or without oak aging. Think barbecue.

BAGA: A great grape so searingly tannic that it may never have a chance to be pursued for its greatness. In the sandy soils of Bairrada, in north central Portugal, it can produce wine that will live for decades.

BARBERA: Italy's most widely planted red grape produces credible wine wherever it is grown and deserves greater acclaim. Yet its lack of commercial success is based solely upon its reputed short shelf life and ignores its excellence with a variety of foods and plethora of fruit flavors. If that is to change, at least in America, it will have to be soon, because vineyards are being uprooted.

BONARDA: Several different varieties are grown under the same name in northern Italy. But Bonarda has found fertile soil in Argentina, where it's widely planted. It's thick and juicy but herbaceous in underripe years.

CABERNET FRANC: Ubiquitous and invisible, this is the John Q. Public of wine. Pomerol and St.-Emilion, regions which have created Merlot's international fame, are just as dependent upon Cabernet Franc. Its fruit-basket, cherry flavors can be utterly delicious but are often marred by herbaceousness and sometimes leather smells.

Oddly, regions as disparate as Italy, California, and the Loire Valley tend to show the herbal side of the wine, while Bordeaux can make lovely, textured red wine with multivalent fruits and good longevity. Certainly, Cheval Blanc, which is more than half Cabernet Franc, provides proof enough that the grape is truly noble and age-worthy.

The leafy side of Cabernet Franc grows even greener in cooler climates, yet Washington State appears to be an excellent spot for it. While the Cabernets of that area can be too herbal, most Cabernet Francs are delicious. In the eastern United States, New York and Virginia have had good success with the grape. The herbal northern Italian wines labeled simply as Cabernet are more likely to be composed of Cabernet Franc than Cabernet Sauvignon.

CABERNET SAUVIGNON: This grape makes wine that is invariably intense in black cherry, cedar, and black pepper flavors. In cooler vineyards such as in Bordeaux (in bad vintages) and New Zealand, the wine can be herbaceous and stingy; in warmer spots (Bordeaux in good vintages, California, and Australia), it's lush in youth and yet long-lived.

The grape's primacy in Bordeaux is surprisingly recent; more common two hundred years ago were Petit Verdot and Cabernet Franc, which is Cabernet Sauvignon's progenitor. As with Chardonnay, this is an adaptable grape that has been used in virtually every vineyard region in the world. And while it has been co-opted in places from Paarl to Perth, it responds less comfortably to the plethora of styles that Chardonnay has allowed.

Expensive Cabernet Sauvignon is a game of extraction and oak. The more, the better, it would seem. Generally speaking, the American-led wine marketplace has viewed Cabernet-making as a pursuit of power. And Cabernet's virtue in this is that, unlike Zinfandel, it does not automatically swap power for elegance.

A good winemaker working with ripe Cabernet grapes can create explosive and mouth-filling fruit without necessarily allowing searing tannins or absurdly heady alcohol. Yet Cabernet's earlier fame was as a component of Claret, the British term for mild and simple Bordeaux.

CARIGNAN: The world's most prolific red-grape vine offers fat and friendly wine wherever it's grown—in California, Spain (in Cariñena), Italy, or across the breadth of southern France. When the vines are older, it can be almost remarkable, though not long in finish or lifespan. Black cherry, raspberry, and dusty earth describe the best versions.

CARMENERE: Bottled only in Chile, it arrived there in the mid-nineteenth century from Bordeaux. The grape needs to be planted in warm sites to taste clean and crisp like the best crème de cassis. Though rich plum and cherry flavors are abundant, there is a leafy note that's spicy in warm vintages and green and hard in tough ones.

OPPOSITE: One of America's greatest Cabernet vineyards is at Robert Mondavi's Oakville estate.

CHAMBOURCIN: A hybrid with success in the United States and Australia, it can be purple and rich in texture, with blueberry and raspberry notes and a somewhat leafy finish.

CINSAUT: It helps produce Tavel Rosé, possibly the world's greatest rosé, as well as adding black pepper and leafy, aromatic notes to Côtes du Rhône.

COUNOISE: An obscure grape until recently, when the famed Château de Beaucastel began publicizing its use of the grape in its Châteauneuf-du-Pape blend, to which it adds very lovely red-berry flavors.

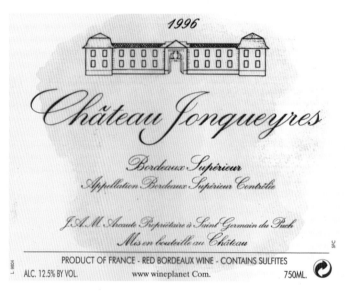

LEFT: Dolcetto has only recently graduated from café carafes to respected bottles. RIGHT: Though composed primarily of Merlot, this Bordeaux estate, like most others, eschews varietal labeling.

CRIOLLA: Argentina's primary grape is called País in Chile and in both countries it's declining in use, thankfully. This leaves room for higher quality grapes.

DOLCETTO: Until recent times, Italy's "little sweet one" was used as a table grape as frequently as the base for wine. It has now become popular although only within the vineyards of Italy's Piedmont. The wine is rarely offered sweet but is intensely fruity nonetheless with plum and blueberry flavors.

GAGLIOPPO: It is a strangely maligned grape, suffering from the general prejudice against anything from southern Italy. It's producing some lovely wines in Calabria under the name of Cirò.

GAMAY: This Beaujolais-based grape can make lovely, seductive wines with great consistency, but greatness is something little Gamay rarely achieves. Its commercial success earns it little respect among wine drinkers, although a handful of Beaujolais producers can create wines resembling red Burgundy in the right soils and from the right vintage.

GRENACHE (GARNACHA): It is a grape that seems less than important to new wine drinkers yet accounts for an enormous portion of the world's vineyards, making it the second most planted grape worldwide. The most common iterations are France's Côtes du Rhône and Châteauneuf-du-Pape, and it's a major component in Rioja and other great Spanish wines. California has vast plantings of the grape—so much so that Gallo was compelled years ago to make not just White Zinfandel but White Grenache.

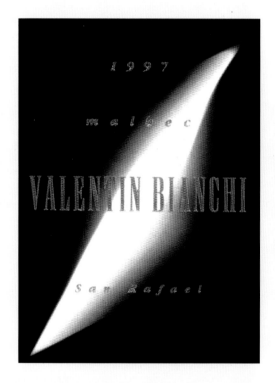

The flavors of strawberry, black and white pepper, and cherry are common. There is a dessert version called Banyuls that is the world's greatest wine with chocolate, and tastes more like chocolate than chocolate.

GRIGNOLINO: A rose-colored wine with the pretensions of a more robust red wine. It's quite tasty with lemon flavors, strawberry tartness, and a floral note.

KADARKA: Another obscure grape deserving more attention, this one is grown in Hungary, Austria, Romania, and Bulgaria (where it's called Gamza). Its frequent title in Hungary is Bull's Blood, so you probably get the hint: it's not a light wine.

LEFT: While most Malbecs don't age well for more than ten years, some do. Most are delicious when young. RIGHT: Few California Merlots are worth the price but some, like Draxton, are lush and tasty.

LAGREIN: This grape produces richly textured, plum- and cherry-flavored reds (and a few rosés) from the Alto Adige in northern Italy.

LEMBERGER: This grape produces wine similar to Dolcetto but with a trace more tannin and jammier fruit. It's offering tasty wines in its native Austria (as Blaüfrankisch) and Washington State (in addition to a few other places). It's known as Limberger in Germany but for many of us that's a cheese.

MALBEC (COT): It is a grape on the decline in Bordeaux and the wider area of southwest France, though it was once a much bigger player. While its style is fat and simple in most areas, Cahors (France) and Argentina show that the grape can be multilayered and even complex in certain sites with black cherry, plum, and slight earth notes.

MAVRODAPHNE: A Greek grape producing good (and sometimes sweet) red wine with aging ability. It's also known as Mavrud in Bulgaria where it produces very good, rich wine.

MERLOT: Generally this grape produces wine that is both soft and rich and, whether in Italy, America, or Australia, new plantations are growing rapidly. It's more widely planted than Cabernet Sauvignon in Bordeaux and embodies the classic flavors of the region—cherries, herbs, and cedar. Its singular strengths are present on the right bank of Bordeaux but it has been great only intermittently in the rest of the world.

MONTEPULCIANO: An intense and inexpensive red grown mostly in the Abruzzi near the coast of Italy along the Adriatic Sea. It's like a slurry of plum and cherry skins in a wine glass.

MOURVÈDRE: Grown successfully and widely in Spain, Australia, California, and, most important, southern France. It may be less true in the other places, but in the southern Rhône and Provence it's one of the grapes most deserving of the description "earthy." It has a lovely cherry richness but its earthiness is less mushroomy (as with Pinot Noir) and more gamey. For some it's rather off-putting in this version but that character fades with age and reveals a more delicate creature.

Mataro, as the grape has been called in California (Monstrell, in Spain), is less earthy, if slightly less complex. But it is only the lack of will of most producers that has prevented this grape from entering the pantheon of great grapes.

NEBBIOLO: Clearly one of the top ten red grapes in the world, it is still annoyingly intolerant of climates, terroirs, and regions. The fog (nebbia) for which it is named is one of the requirements of this finicky vine, although a long growing season with cold nights and warm days is even more necessary. In the wrong spots (even in Italy), it's light in color, acidic, and seemingly tired, though it can last for years. In the right spots—for example, Italy's Barolo and Barbaresco—it is one of the world's greatest wines and can live and be drinkable for decades.

OPPOSITE: Lemberger grapes.

Light in color, it's redolent with floral notes, and is as earthy as a sweaty vineyard worker. But the flavors from this grape are unlike any other and, for that alone, it deserves a place in the hall of grape greatness.

NORTON: A native American grape producing massive and intense red wines.

PETIT VERDOT: An intense, tannic, and tough grape producing a small fraction of the blends of many classic wines in the Médoc of Bordeaux. Though the fraction is rarely more than 1 percent, some producers insist that its long-lived firmness is integral to the character of their wines. The winemaker of Lafite once told me that without Petit Verdot, Lafite would not be Lafite. It was once widely planted throughout Bordeaux, and may help account for the amazing longevity of nineteenth-century Bordeaux wines.

PINOT MEUNIER: Champagne's dirty little secret is that more vineyards are planted with this so-called lesser grape than with either of the more noble varieties, Chardonnay and Pinot Noir. Some of Champagne's oldest vineyards are Pinot Meunier, yet the producers speak little of it, preferring to limn the fleshiness of Pinot Noir or the longevity of Chardonnay.

But times are changing. The Krugs, whom none can question in matters of quality, proudly speak about their Pinot Meunier. Others may soon be more forthcoming. Pinot Meunier seems to be another of those grapes that are less than impressive from youthful vines, but that age can greatly alter. Old vine Pinot Meunier is not simply fruity and soft (early drinkability has always been its virtue) but rich.

Known as Spätburgunder grapes in Germany, these grapes are commonly called Pinot Noir elsewhere.

PINOT NOIR: This grape makes a wine that can be fragile or long-lived, rich and fruity, or meager and thin, depending upon the region. Most examples show greater consistency these days, with near fruit-basket prettiness being produced in both the New and Old Worlds. Wine books still proffer that Pinot Noir is the great frustration among wines—one may have a great bottle of Burgundy (Pinot Noir's great region) and then search for years for another, similar experience.

Those wine writers need to buy more than one bottle of Burgundy a year. For my money, Pinot Noir is a very good value. I would certainly prefer to drink a fifteen-dollar bottle of American Pinot Noir than a fifteen-dollar bottle of Merlot. In fact, I think I'd prefer the fifteen-dollar bottle of Pinot to a thirty-dollar bottle of Merlot, but writers don't complain about that particular grape, do they?

As usual, beauty is in the mouth of the taster. Burgundy prices have risen, along with everything else, but at a pace that's more horse-drawn buggy than the jet-propelled prices of American Cabernet or Bordeaux. And the vintages of the 1990s have been as kind to Burgundy as they have been cruel to Bordeaux. Bordeaux's price increases are often unjustified, while Burgundy dawdles along behind.

Most crucial, a typical Bordeaux release is far less rare than a Burgundy bottle. Château Margaux may produce thirty thousand cases or more of its excellent wine, while in Burgundy, Henri Lafarge's brilliant Volnay Clos des Chênes has a production equal to 2 percent of that. Guess which costs more?

Regardless of the money involved, the frustration of Pinot Noir is that it seems light and even simple at times, yet is as complicated as a starlet on a movie set. While it rarely carries the weight of Bordeaux, a good vintage requires ten or more years to show its stuff. Those of us in the prediction business have been embarrassed far too often by Burgundy's notorious variability and therein lies the truth. For wine drinkers, Pinot Noir is not too difficult. Rather, Pinot Noir makes fools of those of us who would aspire to perfect prognostication.

We forget that that is a great thing. When wines change, when they vary, when they veer from the course carefully laid out by vintner or wine reviewer, it's part of the most fascinating aspect of wine—it can seem to have a personality. For wine writers, this is too much like being left at the altar, and the result is a heap of tearful scorn.

Having said all that, Pinot Noir in the New World is still very much a work in progress. Though the wines may age in unpredictable ways, they rarely repay aging in the same way as Burgundy. For many New World producers, this will change as the vines age. Although Oregon remains America's greatest hope, it is still less than thirty years old. New Zealand, the new land-mark that is about to appear on the horizon, has only two great vintages under its belt.

Most Pinot Noirs are delicious when young with black cherry and raspberry, currant and plum, and at least a dozen fruits all in elegant balance. Occasionally Pinot Noirs become more exotic and nuanced, and may have the depth common to great Burgundies.

PINOTAGE: It's a South African crossing that was created in 1926, in hopes of making a wine with the best traits of its parents—the grace of Pinot Noir and the consistency of Cinsaut. South Africans achieved the latter but nothing close to the former. Still, Pinotage has been and may soon reclaim its position as the Zinfandel of South Africa. But unlike Zinfandel, its palette runs the gamut from only A to B, and a strong controversy brews over its "true" style.

Traditional Pinotage was light but intense and often smelled of faulty winemaking, with nail polish and shellac aromas overwhelming the curranty fruit. Through clonal selection (and better winemaking), the Pinotage offered now is ripe and succulent, with blueberry and black-berry aromas. Still, some people complain that the lack of faults make it atypical and incorrect.

SAGRANTINO: This is a newly respected grape from Umbria (Italy), which received its DOCG (see Glossary) status in 1995. In the hands of a master, such as Arnaldo Caprai, the wine is pow-erful, sinewy, and very long-lived. But in truth, it is rather brutal in its youth, with its black cherry-plum sweetness overwhelmed by dusty tannins.

SANGIOVESE: This is a grape in transition, although that statement carries less impact than it did ten years ago. Sangiovese is just as dependent upon specific growing conditions as Nebbiolo, yet is more forgiving. Certainly it can be drinkable from a wide variety of sites. California's efforts

PAGES 54-55: Lytton Springs, one of the greatest old sites for Zinfandel in California—and the world. BELOW: Shiraz grapes.

have rarely repaid the effort involved, but Sangiovese throughout central and northern Italy (including Brunello and Chianti) can exist anywhere in a continuum from tasty to great.

The fiascos of old, and the straw baskets named after them, have given way to bottles far better. A minority of producers—about 10 percent—are making great wine from this grape and provide liquid proof that the grape is one of the world's most important. There are a multiplicity of clones and names: Chianti, Brunello di Montalcino, Morellino di Scansano, and Vino Nobile di Montepulciano. Each can be rich with blueberry-plum notes and as tart as a bowl of cherry skins; some taste like nut pie and can age for two decades.

SYRAH: This grape produces wines of great black-fruit intensity and often shows black pepper and smoked meat aromas and flavors. It can age up to twenty years or more, but seems eminently drinkable at any age. Its peppery and meaty character varies greatly from region to region; most of the bottlings from the northern Rhône Valley show these characteristics intensely. But the best producers from these places (Côte-Rotie, Hermitage, St.-Joseph, Crozes-Hermitage, and Cornas) give beautifully lush fruit as well.

Lushness doesn't begin to de-scribe typical efforts with the grape in Australia, where it's called Shiraz. Shiraz is unabashedly fruity and often sweet with the vanilla-coconut flavors of American oak barrels. New plantings are in cooler regions and are less overt and friendly, and simpler, and producers of this style of Shiraz are starting to use French oak barrels for their complex wines.

American Syrah is nowhere near as commercially successful, but can be delightful and even long-lived. Excellent Syrah has been made from Mendocino, in northern California, to Santa Ynez and is limited only by plantings, which are still minimal. Washington State is quickly proving its prowess with the grape.

South Africa has a history of good Syrah from Stellenbosch and Paarl, though the wine is most often as lean and peppery as a moderately priced Côtes du Rhône.

TANNAT: An intense and tannic red wine utilized in southwest France, especially around the town of Madiran.

TEMPRANILLO: The Spanish region of Rioja has carried the torch for this noble but forgotten grape, yet Spain's other great wines are most often based upon it. Experiments with the grape outside Spain have been frustrating, adding to the wine's anonymity. Cherry flavors with some blueberries and low acidity describe its contribution to Rioja, yet it is great in other spots throughout Spain, especially Rebero del Duero.

The grape's best characteristic is its softness and strange durability. Low acidity should connote fragility and lack of longevity. Instead, Tempranillo is always friendly and drinkable, but with uncanny strength. Some zealous Riojan producers have left the wine in barrels for a decade or more. It soaks up the fascinating vanilla of American oak and still expresses fruits like blue plum with sweet black cherry juice.

ZINFANDEL: Italy, especially in Puglia, is beginning to bottle the Primitivo grape (otherwise known as Zinfandel) but America will continue to define this grape for decades. It has a slippery black- and blue-fruit flavor—think of plum and currant jelly—with firm tannins throughout. Most producers find it so juicy that they hit it with a firm dose of American oak barrels, giving it an aromatic, sawdust aroma.

Zinfandel was described as a chameleon in 1984's *Book of California Wine*. In it, essayist (and Ridge Vineyards winemaker) Paul Draper famously noted that Zinfandel enjoyed commercial life as a white wine, a rosé, a light Claret-style wine, a richer, more Cabernet-like wine, a high-alcohol blockbuster, a dessert wine, and a Port.

Most Zinfandel is still offered in its pink version, but that style's days appear numbered. Proprietary rosés, less-expensive blends of grapes, may capture this shrinking market and many other red grapes offer rosés that are richer and more elegant. But Zinfandel lovers owe white Zinfandel a lot; it saved Zinfandel vines from certain destruction in the 1980s, when Chardonnay threatened to take over the world.

Today, the old-vine Zinfandel vineyards are disappearing regardless of the renewed interest and strong prices—victims of greed, grape fashion, and old age. It remains to be seen if young vines will offer the same quality as the great old Zinfandels of California's past.

4

Pride of Places

the new world

THE WORLD'S GETTING BIGGER

We're better at growing grapes for wine than we have ever been. Because of this, and because people like to drink wine, vineyards of quality are popping up all over the world. At the same time, the lousy ones are disappearing due to competition.

The vinifera vine thrives in a fairly limited latitudinal range, so each grape tends to be planted in just a few places. Nonvinifera varieties are planted in those sites where vinifera does not thrive. Still the ability of wine tasters to identify wines' origins in blind tastings proves, if nothing else, that wine cannot help but reveal its place of origin in its flavor.

THE CULTURE OF AUTHENTICITY

Any wine drinker who becomes passionate about wine, has seen that there is an authentic character to the good wines of a particular region. That often becomes the overriding reason to buy and drink the wine again.

The following profiles of the important vineyards and regions in each country seek to explain how geographic origin impacts the flavor, not for blind-tasting purposes (it's a cheap parlor trick anyway), but to help the buyer predict a wine's flavor and style.

LOCATION, LOCATION, LOCATION OR PEOPLE, PEOPLE, PEOPLE

The vineyard or origin of a wine will never be more important than the integrity of the wine producer. A lousy winemaker will make lousy wines anywhere, and it's pretty hard to appreciate anything about the wine, much less a tiny detail like the flavors that identify the region.

NORTH AMERICA

THE UNITED STATES

From the beginning, America was not about wine. Leif Eriksson, who was supposed to have named this continent Wineland, likely landed only in present-day Newfoundland. If he tasted "grapes" they were probably cranberries, as it was too far north for vines.

The rest of America was jumbled up in vines. The continent is home to over half of the world's known grapevine species but these grapes were not used for wine. They were eaten, and the table grapes still consumed today are most often native American types or hybrids.

Being a mobile people, the lighter the baggage, the better, and distillate is as light as it gets. Partly for this reason, wine has been less popular in America than in most any other status-conscious culture. To the rest of the world, wine predated spirits by a thousand years or more. For Americans, they more or less arrived at the same time.

But the other issue is that vinifera vines planted by the colonists died from mildew and Pierce's Disease. Native American vines gave wines only the locals could love, since the indigenous grapes had an aroma pejoratively described as foxy. Ongoing experimentation with hybrids was proof of the grape's continuing attraction to farmers eager to create a crop base more diverse than ubiquitous tobacco, cotton, and sugar cane.

It has been only in the last one hundred fifty years that we've been able to create an American wine industry, based upon grafted European vines and hybrids. One of the earliest of these was the Catawba—a hybrid that remains indispensable today. Its first notable site was in the District of Columbia's Georgetown and President Thomas Jefferson, an oenophile, pronounced it "a fine wine of high flavor."

Sparkling Catawba was one of the first American wine successes, and by the 1850s vineyards near Cincinnati were producing and selling 50,000 bottles each year. At about the same time, German immigrants in Missouri were fashioning good wines from the Norton grape and one Philadelphia writer, Charles Brace, called the Missouri wines superior to anything he found in California.

New York's first efforts date from this period. Isabella, a hybrid bred on Long Island, was soon grown in the other New York vineyard areas, near the Hudson River, in Chautauqua County, and around the Finger Lakes, following the Civil War.

The larger public might still have been resistant, but here, too, sparkling wine became the focus and the unusual aromas of the native and hybrid grapes were mitigated by that style. By the 1890s, commercial winegrowing was thriving in about a dozen states. And the introduction of new hybrids, with fanciful names such as Duchess, Elvira, Diamond, and especially Concord, sustained the industry.

But diseases and pests were often deadly to the new hybrids, almost as much as they had been to vinifera vines. As bad as their ravages were in America, in the 1850s and 1860s mildew and phylloxera were inadvertently exported to Europe and devastated the vineyards. Faced with the death of their vineyards, the Europeans experimented with American vines and roots. It was quickly proven that phylloxera could not destroy American vines. By grafting European vines onto American roots, the growers created a crop that survived the infestation of phylloxera. Indeed, some of the hybrid vines survived as well, and are still widely planted. But the grafting process took half a century to be completed throughout the world. The disruption of the wine supply allowed new regions and even new beverages easy access to the world marketplace.

So while spirits producers were taking advantage of the devastation of phylloxera to loosen wine's grip upon the world market, Americans had a different mindset, based upon the new vines and wines being produced. Suddenly they had a reason to make, and drink, their own wine. Naturally the rest of the New World had an opportunity to grow its wine production as well. This pertained to no place more than California.

Before and following the annexation of the New Mexico Territory in 1848, mission vineyards such as San Gabriel, San Jose, and San Diego, among others, provided wine mostly for brandy. By the 1850s that landscape was changing. The vineyards in and around Los Angeles, as well as plantings in Cucamonga and Riverside, soon provided a glut of wine that hampered that industry. Most of those vineyards no longer exist, victims of a scourge known then as Anaheim Disease. Today this bacteria, which is again threatening California vineyards, is called Pierce's Disease.

In the nineteenth century, the destruction stopped at Santa Barbara; vineyards in northern California were growing. Interestingly, many of them were initially planted to hybrids. The influx of settlers during the Gold Rush helped create and support vineyards that endure today in the high Sierras, and in Sonoma, Contra Costa, Santa Clara, and San Joaquin counties.

California's growth was fed by a steady influx of wine-proficient immigrants, though many in the United States would attempt to limit immigration from any but northern European countries. To this day, the West Coast wine business is supported by immigrant labor, nowadays from Mexico, and it's still a political hot potato.

The End of an Industry

Prohibition was class warfare in the guise of politics. The transformation of cities into slums, wrought by the acquisition and concentration of wealth following the Industrial Revolution, created a displaced and impoverished working class. The ready availability of cheap spirits helped fuel the maelstrom of poverty and loss. The wealthy class saw no great risk to its own privileges in limiting the rights of the underclass, and Prohibition began by limiting only spirits.

The first sites of total Prohibition were in nonurban locales spurred by the urban horror stories from a lurid, nineteenth-century press. There were numerous authorities pressing for an end to "demon alcohol": doctors, social theorists, ambitious politicians, and suffragettes. Health advocates were most often involved; Dr. Welch's grape juice was purposely nonalcoholic. Indeed, stable, nonfermenting grape juice was made commercially possible by the writings of Louis Pasteur, who devoted the bulk of his career to developing our modern understanding of fermentation. Pasteur would probably not have been pleased to know that his ideas aided one of the vocal opponents of wine.

The popular view of the working class's alcohol consumption.

Despite the early victories, local laws provided only patchwork success for the Prohibitionists. Compton, today home to West Coast hip-hop, was founded as a teetotaling community, but the vineyards of the Los Angeles area nearby produced wine unabated.

A nationwide Prohibition would have no such obstacle to its goal of social engineering. The Temperance forces acted as independent promoters, supporting any Democratic or Republican politician willing to further their goal. A half century of anti-alcohol propaganda yielded a quick ratification of the Eighteenth Amendment. The outcome was a nation of lawbreakers, as drinkers refused to obey the law.

A thirsty public fueled an illegal whiskey industry from which criminals benefited. Tabloids and dime-store novels depicted tales only slightly more lurid than reality and organized crime's horrific involvement helped change public sentiment towards Prohibition's "noble experiment."

The Long Road Back

When, in 1933, President Franklin Delano Roosevelt celebrated the repeal of Prohibition by mixing a martini at the stroke of midnight, December sixth, he was so adept at making one, it was as though he had been making them all along.

Wine would not reappear on the cultural radar until the 1950s. A more educated and well-traveled public sought the well-known wines produced in Europe. American wine marketers, mindful of the successes of the nineteenth century, took on the wine names that had worked then. So Chablis, Burgundy, Rhine, Champagne, Chianti, and Claret graced wine labels in the '50s and '60s.

Today there is an abundance of good news and excellent wine emanating from states not only on the West Coast, but also in the Midwest, the Southwest, and along the eastern seaboard.

California's Dominance

The most obvious home for wine today, and the site of 90 percent of America's production, is California. The state's supremacy was likely due to its agricultural base and its moderate climate, but it wasn't manifest destiny. California's winegrowers earned their ownership of the nation's wine industry by focusing upon both local and national markets, by constant experimentation with viticulture and vinification, and by having the good fortune to use familiar, respected vinifera vines.

When Robert Mondavi and others began promoting California wine as a purely varietal endeavor in the early 1960s, they consequently simplified wine for Americans. This helped fuel California's success above all other regions and set the stage for wine's astronomic increase in sales.

CALIFORNIA

However, even in the twenty-first century, wines labeled red, white, or rosé, or even Burgundy and Chablis, the so-called generics, account for 35 percent of all American wine sales. This number drops between 3 and 7 percent every year. The next step for Californians is to accomplish what the Europeans have done: to identify certain grapes in certain regions as possessing specific flavors and aromas, ones which the buyer will seek out at higher and higher prices.

To many producers, it is far too early to begin this process. France has had about one thousand years of experience; we probably deserve more than the thirty or so expended thus far on a wide selection of grapes and styles.

But as of this writing AVAs (American Viticultural Areas) number 137. Though there is no claim that certain varieties prosper in certain AVAs, focusing upon the grapes planted in any AVA says volumes about its future direction.

Regions in the South and Central Coast

Throughout southern California, cooler climate grapes, especially white ones, prevail. In **Temecula** good Chardonnay, Sauvignon Blanc, and Gewürztraminer lead the way with white grapes but Zinfandel, Petite Sirah, and Syrah can be delicious, too.

Toward the ocean from Santa Barbara are two of the best Chardonnay/Pinot Noir regions in America—the **Santa Maria** and **Santa Ynez Valleys**. Rhone varieties are showing great promise as well, and Sauvignon Blanc has an excellent track record here.

The Regions of the Central Coast

The **Paso Robles** area offers enormous promise from virtually every grape grown in America. Though the region has produced few of America's best wines, in the future we should expect great Rhone variety wines as well as other excellent reds.

The large **Edna Valley** makes good cool climate reds and whites but may suffer from a lack of experimentation, as it has only a few owners.

The **Monterey** AVA is massive and contains a number of excellent white-wine sites, as well as a few good red ones. Within the numerous AVAs on the Central Coast are some of America's best Chardonnay, Pinot Noir, and Cabernet Sauvignon sites. Of particular historical import is the **Santa Cruz Mountains** AVA; as far back as the 1940s, brilliant Cabernets have been grown here, though housing developments will likely supplant all but the best-known vineyards in the next decade.

The Regions from the Central Valley to the Mountains

The **Central Valley** is a literal hothouse of general produce, including boring wine, but in the **Clarksburg** and **Lodi** AVAs at the north end of the Central Valley (as well as the nearby **Dunnigan Hills** and **Merritt Island** AVAs), very good wine is produced routinely.

East of San Francisco are two of California's least-heralded but trustworthy AVAs— **Contra Costa** (site of older Zinfandel and Rhône-variety vines) and **Livermore Valley** (very good Bordeaux-style reds and whites).

The **Sierra Foothills** contain some of California's oldest vineyards, with the local Zinfandel only lately receiving the acclaim it has long deserved. Due to the heat, red varieties dominate here.

California's North Counties—Napa County

Napa Valley's primacy in the collective mind of the wine-buying public is based upon certain star wineries. It's a tendency that began at the end of the nineteenth century and that continues today as each new Cabernet-based winery offers its own version of a two-hundred-dollar bottle of bizarrely limited production. Robert Parker anoints the wine (correctly, I must admit) and the winery is off to the bank.

This illustration from an 1880s' California winegrower's guide shows the state's newfound enthusiasm for wine.

This tendency has created the Balkanization of Napa Valley. If smaller and smaller parcels of highly allocated wine can fetch ridiculous dollars, then why not? These sorts of wines are stunning and concentrated examples of what California can do as well or better than any other place. With mouth-crushing fruit and intensely scented oak aromas, these are wines no one could possibly miss. That makes them quintessentially American—they have power without elegance.

But rather than paint all wines here with the same massive brush, let's consider that the wines that receive praise from the lovers of power are—surprise, surprise—powerful. Those of us who love elegance should stick up for our own.

Though the hand of the winemaker has the greatest influence here, as in all places, the regional differences in Napa County, and even within Napa Valley, are distinct. Soils in northern California are very old and quite disparate from site to site.

The mountain vineyards produce very extracted wines and account for many of the recent stars of the area. **Howell Mountain**, comprising part of the eastern rim of Napa Valley, generally produces wines that need taming and the best of these are very long-lived; they can also age in frustrating fits and starts.

Stag's Leap looks like a mountain and its bowl of vineyards below towering peaks forms another part of the eastern edge of the valley. The late afternoon sun bakes the grapes to a rich, jammy stew and Stag's Leap wines are generally a hedonistic delight. As such, some believe them to lack structure, but that's a bit like scrutinizing the gift horse.

Mount Veeder lies across the valley from Stag's Leap, and those making wine from grapes baked on its high hills had better learn to "ripen tannins," as one well-known winemaker here puts it. California wines are never at a loss for tannin, and the challenge here, as it is on most hilltop sites, is to make the wine fleshier and de-emphasize the forbidding structure.

Spring Mountain vineyards can share the toughness of Mount Veeder but the hillside vineyards that stretch from north of Oakville to Calistoga share little else in common, except some

Though it's a simplistic view, the warm and sunny Napa Valley is synonymous with great wine for most Americans.

are truly great. Diamond Mountain is being petitioned as an AVA and lays claim to a fairly short history of very good, sinewy mountain wines.

The Napa Valley AVA itself can comprise any of these areas but mostly includes the valley-floor vineyards. The center portion of Napa has been parceled into **Yountville** in the south, **Rutherford** in the center, and **Oakville**, all AVAs in search of a purpose.

Rutherford has fame on its side; the "Rutherford dust" flavor is a bona fide textural and aromatic element that occurs in some, but not by any means all, of the better wines from this spot. But this is no different than in any other country; lines of wine demarcation are first and foremost political in nature.

The other valleys within Napa County include Pope Valley (not yet an AVA) and **Chiles Valley** (rich Chardonnay and Sémillon, and good red Bordeaux varieties), **Wild Horse Valley**, and **Atlas Peak** (so-so wines thus far).

PAGES 66-67: Northern Sonoma County produces some of California's richest red wines. ABOVE: Hand-picking grapes in Carneros, California.

The name **Los Carneros** enshrines the region's past as a grazing zone for its once-ubiquitous sheep. It's now the home of Napa Valley's only cool climate vineyards though, in truth, more of Los Carneros's acreage is found in Sonoma County than in Napa County.

Forty years ago, this region was thought to be too cold to produce a consistently commercial crop. Thirty years ago, the few vineyards here, such as Bacigulupi and Winery Lake, were growing highly prized grapes. Today, of course, the place is planted from windy hill to windy hill, not all of it well placed. Nevertheless, this is good country for Pinot Noir, Chardonnay, and sparkling wine, with occasional Merlot and Cabernet sites thriving.

Sonoma County shares more than Los Carneros with Napa Valley; it is undoubtedly the other well-known wine region of California. Resentment lingers here over the fact that upstart Napa, with less time under its belt, has won the fame game. Yet Sonoma contains more wineries and more vineyards than Napa and succeeds with a greater number of grapes than its more storied neighbor to the east. Whether the grape is a Bordeaux variety or a Rhône grape, and whether a sparkling, still, or dessert wine, Sonoma offers as many or more great choices than Napa.

And when it comes to Pinot Noir and Chardonnay, Sonoma has better wine. With many of Carneros's vineyards in Sonoma, Carneros Chardonnay is a benchmark. But the Chardonnays and Pinot Noirs from the western portion of Sonoma are as good as any that California has ever produced. For these wines, the proximity to the ocean causes colder all-around temperatures; this gives wines more tartness and longevity.

Green Valley, too, has excellent white wine and sparklers. But it's not only the AVAs close to the ocean that benefit: the **Russian River Valley** and **Chalk Hill** AVAs also experience cold nights courtesy of the ocean air draining up the Russian River and from the Bay. These regions make beautifully balanced wines, whether white or red. Even sun-drenched **Sonoma Mountain** retains good acidity from nighttime air.

Farther to the east, the wines tend to be fatter and reflect the consistently warmer conditions. At the north and eastern ends of the county, in **Dry Creek**, **Alexander**, and **Knights Valleys**, the wines have less overt acidity but can enjoy an almost Stags Leap–like richness of fruit. These wines may not age as well as those from the cooler parts of the county, but who cares? The well-known bottles are delicious.

To the north of Dry Creek Valley is **Mendocino County**. Once home to ranches and head shops, it is now more thoroughly planted to grapes than ever before. Though the vineyards are twice the distance from the ocean as Dry Creek, there are fewer hills blocking the movement of the ocean air inland at night. Grapes from much of Mendocino can show an almost applelike tartness and some of America's best sparkling wines have been produced here.

Lake County was once a region of only a few wineries and vineyards; in only ten years, it has quadrupled its acreage. The region's climate is more moderate than Mendocino and rich wines from nearly every grape grown here have been made.

Delille Cellars, one of the many high-quality, small wine producers in Washington State.

The Specific Northwest

Though Oregon and Washington (and sometimes Idaho) are lumped together as the Pacific Northwest, they are radically different places. Oregon contains two warm-site AVAs—at least warm in comparison to the rest of the state: **Rogue River Valley** and **Umpqua Valley** and a variety of grapes from Gewürztraminer to Merlot have done well here.

The more famous AVA, the **Willamette Valley**, is considered America's promised land for Pinot Noir. Although there are many that dispute Oregon's excellence with the grape, the best producers here make Pinot Noir as good as or better than any in America.

Pinot Gris, too, has shown extremely well in a very short time, yet the wine has rarely shown the kind of richness associated with Alsace Pinot Gris. In reality, producers here should call their wine Pinot Grigio, since it has more in common with the crisp lightness of the Italian version of the grape.

Chardonnay has been a disaster here, but that's changing as Burgundian clones are allowed into the state. These Dijon clones, as they are called, are radically transforming Oregon Chardonnay into a lovely, rich wine.

Oregon's northeast corner holds one of the Northwest's most exciting AVAs, the **Walla Walla Valley**. Though its fame derives from Washington State bottlings, the region is growing more quickly on the Oregon side. Merlot, Cabernet Franc, Cabernet Sauvignon, Syrah, and even Sangiovese are very promising here.

The disparity between Walla Walla and the Willamette Valley is explained by the Cascade Mountains, which act as a barrier for cool ocean air and moisture. The Willamette Valley lies on the ocean side of the Cascades and is correspondingly cool and wet, often during harvest. For this reason, Oregon Pinot Noir can be great one vintage and so-so the next, not unlike Burgundy itself.

Walla Walla and all of Washington State's best vineyards are to the east of the Cascades. They are dry, hot in summer, and cool at night, and enjoy long growing seasons and consistently produce extracted, powerful, and long-lived wine. The downside is that they often don't enjoy the flattering fruit of California wine, with which they are often compared. And the winters can be deadly to Washington's vines; in fact, many vineyardists allow each vine to grow two separate trunks. With a killing frost estimated to occur every five to seven years, growers have found that one of the two trunks usually survives.

Though Washington State is a land of excellent value wines, too many sites are planted in places too cold to consistently ripen Bordeaux varieties. Today, Washington State's planted acres equal Napa Valley. A relatively small percentage of those vineyards will often produce great wine. Those vineyards around Canoe Ridge, in other favored parts of the **Yakima** and **Columbia Valleys** and especially Red Mountain, a small non-AVA portion of the Columbia Valley, are consistent producers of great wines.

With only about two decades of wine production under their belts, vineyards in Washington and Oregon have proven that they can make wines as great as any from California.

The Northeast—Following the Waters

Until the 1950s, no sane wine grower thought that vinifera had a com-mercial future in the Northeast. That's when New York vintner Dr. Konstantin Frank took the Finger Lakes industry to task for avoiding vinifera. At the time, and for years afterward, he was laughed at. Today, all will concur that, in fact, Dr. Frank was a visionary. The temperature-moderating effect of the

Finger Lakes allows a smart grower to retain most if not all of their vinifera vines, regardless of the harshness of some winters.

The thread winding through all these vineyards is that throughout the Northeast and Great Lakes areas, the proximity to water (whether the lakes or the ocean), combined with sufficient shelter from violent weather, allows vinifera to flourish. Good wines are being produced from Ohio to Michigan and western New York, because of the nearness to the Great Lakes. On New York's Long Island, excellent vinifera wines (especially Cabernet Franc and Merlot) are grown in climates ameliorated by the ocean.

But a number of other regions throughout the country have offered good to excellent wine; if you're an open-minded type, try a Colorado Lemberger, a New Mexico sparkler (Château-Gruet), a Missouri Norton, or a Virginia Barbera. Vinifera is showing a surprising ability to survive in many parts of America and the rest of the country is beginning to understand how hybrids can create very good wines when handled skillfully. In the success of wines such as these, surely American consumers will soon be better informed about the quality from the states outside the Left Coast, and this awareness will increase wine's visibility in American life.

MEXICO

There are some very good wines being produced in Mexico, albeit in an ocean of lackluster or terrible wines. The country has massive vineyards but most grapes grown here are destined to become the world's most popular brandy, El Presidente. The older vineyards are clustered in the state of Sonora, all for brandy, while decent grapes have been grown northwest of Mexico City in the states of Aguascalíentes and Zacatecas. Most wine grapes are grown in Baja, and the tiny Valle de Guadalupe is having some exceptional results.

South of the entertaining squalor that is Tijuana, a small group of wineries (Monte Xanic, Château Camou and, sometimes, Santo Tomas) are setting a bar unlikely to be met by any of the other wineries in the area in the immediate future. Try Monte Xanic's Kristal (a Sauvignon Blanc/Sémillon blend), or their Cabernet Franc and Cabernet Sauvignon wines. As the valleys here are open to the ocean, the heat of Baja is mitigated, and a dedicated winery like this can make very good wines.

CANADA

With improved hybrid-growing techniques, vineyards in Quebec and Ontario are far more likely to succeed than they were when wines were first attempted here. But if good vinifera wine is made in New York State (and it is), there is no reason that the southern boundaries of Canada cannot do the same.

But while winegrowing here is nearly two centuries old, the industry has only begun to chase after the quality of which it is capable. Ontario has the longest commercial history, but much of the story of Canadian wine is simply the history of a protected industry. The work of the last ten years is strong evidence that Canadian wineries can make very good and even excellent wines.

But, though this is even more true in British Columbia, the favored sites there are too few in number and size to allow a large-scale, high-quality wine industry, one that could support a strong export market. British Columbia has been more radically transformed by the introduction of vinifera varieties in the last two decades. While the red wines are still of mostly regional interest, many of the whites are simply delicious, so Canada's best wines stay home. With solid Gewürztraminer, Pinot Gris, Pinot Blanc, and Riesling here, excellent wines are in evidence in the Similkameen and Okanagan valleys of southern British Columbia, but only people there and in America's Pacific Northwest have a chance to buy them.

SOUTH AMERICA

The best vineyards in Chile are never far away, rarely more than thirty miles, from the Andes Mountains.

There's no question that it's time for South America to exert itself on the world wine scene. For too long, the wines have been "good values" which, in an era of easy income, is the kiss of grandma. The reds have received decent praise while the whites have been no better than troublesome. Though change is the constant in wine, some changes afoot are altering the wine landscape here forever. No change that comes after will be quite as dramatic.

CHILE

Some parts of the country have been producing wine for over five hundred years, but the modern Chilean wine industry is being born in front of our eyes. The 1980s and 1990s saw a strong drop in production, with a slight increase in vineyard acreage. Contrast that with Argentina, where acreage is not much greater, but that country's yields are over four times that of Chile's. For good to great wine to be produced, wine industries must first abandon the excessive yields (ten to twenty tons per acre!) that filled the cups in the taverns so cheaply.

While Chile's commitment to quality dates back to those decisions made ten or so years ago, it is with the 1999 vintage that we were able to clearly see the fruits of that labor. But Chile's first challenge lay in discovering what grapes they had already planted.

Sizable plantings of Sauvignon Blanc and Merlot here have been shown to be two other grapes, Sauvignonasse and Carmenere, respectively. The result will be to increase plantings of true Sauvignon Blanc and to learn to make great wine from the nearly lost Bordeaux variety, Carmenere. The new sites for Sauvignon Blanc, often nearer the coast than the historical sites, are already proving excellent with Chardonnay and Gewürztraminer.

Carmenere, as well as the rest of the potentially or already excellent red grapes (Merlot, Cabernet Sauvignon, Syrah), need warmer spots. Chile's earlier practice was to ape the ripening cycles of Bordeaux, to which some thought it shared an affinity. Nothing could be further from the mark. Chile is blessed by an outrageously long growing season, but needs every bit of it to ripen flavors in red grapes. Growers have learned to allow the grapes to ripen until there is almost no acidity left, and then to add acid to the wines, not unlike growers in California. When a good vintage arrives, the result is a beautiful, textured, aromatic wine. However, it is not long-lived. The real moral of this story is that Chile is an easy place to grow grapes, but a tough place to make great wine.

Most wine books will tell you that one vintage is the same as another in Chile. Some of them still say that about Australia and America—and they're just as wrong. Purchase only ripe vintages from Chile, and you will find some of the most delicious, inexpensive wines in the world. Even with certain producers leading the charge in pricing, excellent wines abound in the under-twenty-dollar category.

And the paradigm will, as we used to say in the 1990s, shift. Growers are siting vineyards near the coast (Casablanca Valley) or nestled in the vertiginous slopes of the Andes (Aconcagua Valley). The best vineyards in those places are offering wines of better ageability. Spots in Maipo Valley, even in the coolish Rapel Valley (such as the Apalta Valley) are very exciting.

ARGENTINA

As Carmenere is for Chile, so Malbec is Argentina's own grape to define and with which to define itself to consumers. Though Malbec is also grown in and around Bordeaux and parts of California, only in Argentina and in a little place called Cahors in southwest France has Malbec shown greatness.

The country has long been one of the world's top consumers of wine and is number five in production in the world. Its potential is greater than Chile, at least in terms of quantities of

A U S T R A L I A

very good wine, but recently it has lagged behind in quality. Still high-quality producers such as Valentin Bianchi, Norton, Canepa, Alta Vista, Navarro Correas, and Weinert are pushing the pack toward excellence.

Here, too, more internationally styled winemaking is creating wines that are not the long-term agers made before, but are clearly better wines regardless. And though many old Malbec vines were uprooted ten and twenty years ago, there is a newfound respect for the grape here and abroad.

Throughout the vast Mendoza, looking west toward Mount Aconcagua, mountainside vineyards are showing the quality nascent here. Chardonnay, Cabernet Sauvignon, and Argentina's other unusual variety, Bonarda, are joining Malbec as good to excellent wine producers. Cooler sites, recently rediscovered, such as San Rafael and Tupungato, benefit from proximity to the Andes in elevation and longevity of growing season. In the next ten years, the pursuit of greatness in South America will be a horse race between the cool sites of Chile and Argentina.

AUSTRALASIA

AUSTRALIA—UP IN DOWN UNDER

The story of the land Down Under provides as optimistic a look at wine's present and future as any country can offer. Like California, the wine industry was founded by British and German immigrants in the mid-1800s. The wines were destined for community use, as well as certain ready markets of fortune seekers, chasing purported mineral wealth. But in Australia, the "noble experiment" of Prohibition was not visited upon the wine industry in the same draconian manner as in America.

The result was to some degree a negative. By the 1950s, the country's wine industry had settled into standardized beverage production. When the wine boom hit here in the '60s, arriving just shortly after it hit the rest of the New World, the wine industry responded with larger containers. "Bag in box" (wine in a box), to this day, is a big factor in the Australian wine industry. On the other hand, the bags in their boxes contain far better wine than any in American boxes. Because of this and other more entrenched reasons, wine does not carry quite the snob appeal (and social barriers) that it does in America.

Not Hot but Cool

Australia's success at farming for flavor bred a generation of wine drinkers. Today, Aussies consume three times per capita what Americans consume. There must still be room for growth because they also consume four times as much beer. That's one of the many reasons why I love Australia.

But the most fascinating part is that the great Australian wine juggernaut (or so it must seem to struggling Californians, Chileans, Argentians, and, especially, beleaguered South Africans) is preparing to reconstruct itself again.

The success of their wine industry has been built upon two concepts: warm-climate vineyards, and varietal and regional blends. Traditional sites, such as those in the Hunter Valley, much of the Barossa, and areas throughout Victoria, the south, and the famed Coonawarra region, are warm places. This is not to suggest that they are greatly inferior to other, cooler areas. Napa Valley, too, is a warm place. But warm sites offer rich, generous flavor. They offer early drinking wines. Warm sites do not necessarily make wines of great structure or longevity.

What if the cooler sites were to be pursued? In the last ten years, producers have begun to say why not, and to seek out cooler, more challenging sites. So places in Western Australia such as Margaret River or Frankland, cooler spots along the coast (Geelong or Mornington Peninsula), and more commonly, vineyards at greater elevations—along the foothills of Adelaide and above the Barossa Valley—are the new frontier. The new vineyards of the last ten years already offer convincing proof that Australian wine is far from peaking.

Blend, Whip, or Purée?

Australia is a land of realists being overwhelmed by optimists. The successes of the past twenty years and the groundwork laid assure twenty years of greater successes. But the industry is still ruled by a handful of gargantuan wine companies. Unlike similar-scale wineries in America, these wineries have often been at the proverbial slicing edge of winemaking and winegrowing.

While the Hunter Valley is considered to be hot and wet, typical of most of Australia's vineyards, its landscape is less wet than semi-arid.

Yet, eventually, large companies act as agents against change. The lifeblood of the wine business, more so than any other business, is the small winery, and at the moment they are sprouting like fistfights in an outback bar. But remember that the Australian wine business is built not only upon bag in box, but upon its corollary, the blend.

Bin This and That

The prototypical Aussie wine is Bin Number whatever, blending a little bit of great wine from a cool area with a lot of so-so juice from a warm area. The result is a good to very good wine at an extremely good price. This has been the fuel in their tanks at home and abroad.

Proven formulas enforce the formulaic. The success of these blends may prove to be an obstacle to new producers, or to Aussie marketers, or to the mind-sets of consumers.

Bin This May Become That

Old guard wine lovers, trained on Burgundy, Bordeaux, Champagne, and the Rhône, believe that wines must come from a particular place to be great. Still, Australia's greatest wine, from a historical viewpoint only, is Penfolds' Grange, which is a blend of at least two vineyards.

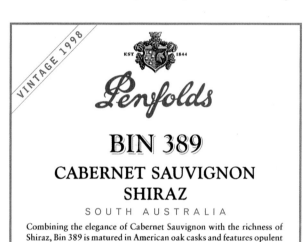

OPPOSITE: New Zealand's long days and many hours of sunshine contribute to the rich intensity of its wines.

NEW ZEALAND

It is inevitable that northern latitudinal wine drinkers think of Australia and New Zealand in the same gulp. Yet, it is more misguided than conflating Washington State and California, and more off course than to imagine Chile and Argentina as separated by a low chain of hills.

Australia built its reputation upon a farm economy unafraid of alcohol, with great value—supplied by warm-climate sites—blended from high yielding vineyards, and brought to market with clever names and silly prices. New Zealand is cold, often wet, isolated, and more cosmopolitan than its situation ought to merit. The wines here are both similar and dissimilar to Australian wines. Both share the rich fruity intensity of the Southern Hemisphere. New Zealand wines are generous to a fault and, in the case of the country's Sauvignon Blanc, some find the flavors of the wine too intense. New Zealand's overall cool climatic conditions, ameliorated by the surrounding Pacific Ocean, give wines excellent acidity despite the fruit intensity.

This means that long-lived wines should be possible in New Zealand, but that has not been seen yet. It's only recently that red grapes have begun to show well at all. Previously, Cabernet Sauvignon was a green and herbal mess. Now Pinot Noir, which once seemed ridiculous here, is expressive and pretty, especially from the South Island. This development is partly due to New Zealand's prominence in the viticultural arena. Many of the world's most interesting vineyard methods have been born or demonstrated here. Not surprisingly, the wines have the bombastic flavors of fresh grapes, as winemakers are eager to show off the purity of their fruit.

The conditions on the North Island should be warmer and easier than in the south but there is more rainfall at harvest. At Marlborough, Canterbury, and even Central Otago, the mountains that bisect the South Island offer a rain shadow and grape planting is exploding there. Today, there are over four hundred wineries on the two islands.

Despite Pinot Noir's new luck, the most likely road forward is with white grapes. Chardonnay and Sauvignon Blanc are clearly proven; Gewürztraminer, Pinot Gris, and Riesling are in the process of offering new routes on New Zealand's road to wine riches.

SOUTH AFRICA

In some ways, South Africa has reflected winemaking before the modern era. Until the early 1980s and the establishment of democracy in the early '90s, much of the red wine here was made in the antiquated style of moderate tannin and high acids from somewhat underripe grapes. The whites were the first to change, as cold fermentation offered fresher, fruitier wines. In 1985, the first commercial Chardonnay was released.

Beautiful Groot Costantia, near the ocean, produces excellent table and dessert wines in South Africa.

It's been a quick transition. Now the majority of the bottled white wines are well made, if not universally interesting. The reds have begun to show the ripeness and oak dominance that expresses the international style. Even Pinotage (see Chapter 3, page 53) is available in the new, cleaner style. And, although sales in the United States are minimal, South African wine has established a beachhead in the United Kingdom and, to a degree, in Europe.

The country's problem was simple; apartheid made it a pariah and isolation allowed mediocrity to reign alongside the racists. When the people here achieved one of the few peaceful transitions to democracy in the world's history, all industries (including wine) sought to create products for export. With established vineyards and excellent growing conditions several hundred miles in every direction from Cape Town, wine was ready to act as an ambassador.

Until the early 1990s, the country's wine industry has been ruled by the KWV, a government-sponsored co-op that provided a place for small farmers and lesser wines. Though the KWV's grip has been loosened, its dominance still hampers progress. But the industry is nonetheless poised to create consistent wines of excellence sometime in the next five years or so.

Aside from Pinotage, all of the usual vines are thriving here, though the boring Chenin Blanc (called Steen) still dominates. The established vineyards of Stellenbosch and Paarl are quite capable of making excellent Cabernet, Syrah, Sémillon, and Sauvignon Blanc and have centuries-old histories to prove it.

Chardonnay and Pinot Noir are the next focus as cooler, coastal regions such as Walker Bay, Mossel Bay, and Elgin are being explored. Fat, California-like Chardonnays have been made in the arid Robertson region. The Coastal Region is a Wine of Origin (or government-approved region) label as specific as Australia's Southeastern Australia designation. That is to say, it's a nearly meaningless appellation comprising hundreds of thousands of acres, most of them far from the coast.

Pride of Places

the old world

F R A N C E

France is the mother of great wine because it has celebrated greatness in wine for far longer than any other country, and with a greater variety of style, origin, and grapes. Other countries make great wines, but no other country has yet made as many diverse, great wines.

CHAMPAGNE—THE REGION

Champagne is arguably the most famous wine in the world; not only does its name stand in for a style of wine (sparkling), the word *Champagne* evokes celebration and conspicuous wealth.

Sparkling wine is the result of allowing wine to ferment in a closed container. As yeast converts grape sugars to alcohol, carbon dioxide is emitted. In typical wine fermentation, the carbon dioxide escapes into the air, but with Champagne and its imitators, the fermentation takes place in the bottle of wine from which it is poured. Producers fill Champagne bottles with table wine and then add a small of amount of yeast and sugar.

A secondary fermentation takes place, but this time the carbon dioxide gas is trapped inside the bottle and makes the wine "sparkling." Wines produced in this manner are labeled as *méthode champenoise* in Champagne and outside Europe. In Europe, the term is *méthode traditionelle* to differentiate sparkling wines made outside the Champagne region.

Father (or Dom) Pierre Pérignon usually gets the credit for Champagne and its method of production, but he is only one of many. The first commercial enterprise specializing in sparkling wine preceded his appointment as winemaker at the Abbey of Hautvillers by hundreds of years. In southern France, barely fifty miles from the Mediterranean, a sparkling wine called Blanquette de Limoux was produced perhaps as long ago as the twelfth century.

While Pérignon did not invent sparkling wine, his true accomplishments are quite remarkable. Others had made a consistently bubbling wine, but his was likely better, as his contemporaries remarked. He helped create the shallow basket press still used today, a lighter and quicker press that creates a wine of more delicacy and, even more important to Pérignon, a white wine from red grapes.

OPPOSITE: Traditionally, Champagne bottles have been placed in pupitres, sandwich-boardlike racks that allow the yeast cells to settle into the neck of the bottle for easier removal.

BRUT: Standard style for each Champagne house; a barely sweet wine, usually with 1 to 1½ percent sugar. Most bottlings are nonvintage, which means that they are blends of as many as five vintages.

BRUT EXTRA: Wine that has very little or no residual sugar. These sorts of wine are bitter in youth but age very well.

EXTRA DRY: A bad translation of the French *demi-sec*, which means "half dry," and refers to a bubbly that is distinctly sweet.

DOUX: A sweet, dessert-style sparkling wine.

VINTAGE CHAMPAGNE: Represents the pinnacle of winemaking and is the best bet for a buyer eager to cellar wine for ten or more years. California's early struggles with quality sparkling wine were created in part by a stubborn insistence upon vintage sparklers; consistency is the reward for blending vintages.

CRÉMANT: Used to refer to Champagne with fewer bubbles (which made it "creamy") but now is the legal term for any French sparkling wine made outside the Champagne region.

Champagne, while most often a white wine, is planted more to red grapes than white grapes. Pinot Noir and Pinot Meunier, both red grapes, account for about two-thirds of the grapes there. But grape juice is usually clear, not colored, and Pérignon's gentle press allowed different grapes, whether red or white, to be blended to create a delicate white sparkling wine.

Pérignon was a proponent of blending: blending of vineyards, of varieties, and of vintages. Blending is at the heart of Champagne's identity and character. It allows wine makers in this cold, northerly region to ameliorate the effects of a weak vintage, and it creates a more complex beverage—one which is likely more consistent of style and flavors. Traditionally, Champagne's benchmark is the "nonvintage" wine, and may be composed of as many as five vintages.

Intermingling vintages allows a younger, or tart, vintage to take on the richer properties of a more mature, or superior, vintage. Perignon's genius was not limited to blending; he helped introduce cork stoppers and heavier glass bottles to France. These improvements made Champagne a more stable and consistent sparkling wine.

Today, regardless of Champagne's historical identity as a place of coronations and celebrations, the sparkling wine made in the Champagne region has earned its primacy of place at the table. The soils of Champagne create a sparkling wine unlike any other: tart and lean in youth, but remarkably complex in maturity.

Those unfamiliar with Champagne's unique character are often surprised that these are wines that can age two or three decades in a good cellar, due to intense acidity. This, too, is the result of extraordinary soils that are deeply laden with chalk—part of a massive plate of chalky earth stretching from spots in Cognac to the white cliffs of Dover (that's why they're white).

BORDEAUX

Bordeaux belonged to Great Britian for exactly three hundred years (1152 to 1452) and it still seems prim and proper today. Bordeaux is a perfect port and was a place of wealth before it was a place of wine. Wine was purchased from established vineyards farther inland and shipped from the quays, stamped Port of Bordeaux. Regardless of its true origin, the wine was known as Bordeaux.

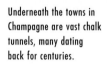

But interesting wine was being produced nearby. The monied paid the Dutch to drain the marshes along the Gironde River and establish vineyards, a symbol of breeding and culture. By the 1700s, the wines from these vineyards up and down the length of the Gironde were commanding the most prestigious prices on the fledgling world wine market. This was partly because the Bordeaux merchants were good at their work and partly because the wines had established themselves as among the world's longest-lived red wines. In a pre-refrigeration era, this made the wines very valuable.

Underneath the towns in Champagne are vast chalk tunnels, many dating back for centuries.

Today, vineyards here are the most expensive in the world. The Bordelais show their mercantile roots by their success at being the world's only wine marketplace where pricing is based solely upon sales of futures. Burgundy cannot make that boast, nor can American soybeans.

Not since 1973 has the group made a false move. In that year, Bordeaux brokers raised prices despite the succession of three bad years and a worldwide recession. The market crashed, briefly, and the Bordeaux buyers ran for cover. Since then, pricing has been extremely savvy while aggressive. Though the 1990s have been as quality-challenged as the 1970s, the Bordelais have made the rest of the wine world look like amateur day traders at a convention of very chummy, establishment insiders.

Despite Bordeaux's shocking elevation in prices in the last ten years, the Asian recession, and a decade of commonplace wines—save 1998 Pomerol/St.-Emilion—the Bordeaux merchants have engineered a near-perfect price increase within the confines of the marketplace's moods. Bordeaux is a business doctoral candidate's dream come true.

These price increases provide a model for the speculative buying and selling of high-end Napa Valley Cabernet. Despite histories no older than three vintages and a couple of superlative Robert Parker reviews, certain

Fear of Champagne

Lots of people think that the bubbles in Champagne speed the alcohol into the bloodstream, but bubbles of carbon dioxide in the bloodstream don't cause drunkenness, they cause death. What causes some people to get drunk more quickly on bubbly? Drinking it far faster than they would a regular table wine.

For those who believe that Champagne exacerbates hangovers, here's the truth: cheap sparkling wine is sweeter and likelier to cause the dehydration that worsens hangovers. So, drink expensive.

California estates can sell for twice that of a Bordeaux first growth. It has been a fairly good decade to California and some labels have shown a rather marked lack of shame in their price increases.

The sweetest irony is that Bordeaux is the both the paradigm and paragon of the international style, a term that describes most wine critics' favorite style of wine. That style is not specific to any place, thus its internationalism, but appeals especially to those newer drinkers most easily seduced by wine-writer hyperbole and by power.

The international style was born of the 1982 Bordeaux vintage. That year, many of us missed the greatness of the wines, but a Washington, D.C. lawyer moonlighting as a wine writer, Robert Parker, called it most accurately when he told us that the wine was the greatest vintage of the previous twenty years. For this he was roundly ridiculed. However, within a year or two, it was clear that he was right.

Thus Parker's reputation was established as the most important wine writer in the world. In truth, he is scrupulous, brilliant, and enormously skilled., if thin-skinned. But, like most of us, his palate is based upon his preferences, and this masquerades as objective wine truth.

Parker is a great asset, but we need more Parkers. His stylistic myopia reflects a genuine love of power and concentration, thus he is a great judge of California red wine, of Bordeaux, and Rhône Valley wines.

Peynaud Mind?

Parker was merely an astute observer. But Emile Peynaud, one of the most important consultants in Bordeaux history, starting from the 1940s, created the style that Parker applauded.

Peynaud was a remarkable figure. His books *Knowing and Making Wine* and *The Taste of Wine* are indispensable reading to a wine lover. Years after the fact, they may not be as scientifically accurate, but are a shockingly concise portrayal of winemaking.

Peynaud demanded that his clients veer away from the traditional path of Bordelais winemaking, which created wines for the cellars of the wealthy. Traditional Bordeaux wines aged well because they were built with some fruitiness, with tannins that resulted from long maceration, and with the acidity from underripe grapes, then the commonplace of Bordeaux grapes. That structure was challenged by Peynaud, for reasons that may always remain a mystery.

Peynaud proposed a structure based upon firm tannins built from maceration as well as new oak barrels and as much ripeness as the season would allow. He believed that this would create a long-lived wine, albeit one likely to please a larger number of drinkers throughout its life. Wines from estates for whom he consulted were criticized for being too California-like in their fruitiness. It is impossible to resist noting that California may well have been Peynaud's model.

Thus the international style creates wines reflecting the supremacy of California-like extraction and emulates Bordeaux's longevity and new French barrel usage. Though the rest of the wine world appears poised to prove its dominance in the style, Bordeaux has benefited most from the public's worship of the style.

Bordeaux fame is also based upon the user-friendly method of categorization called the 1855 Classification. In that year, merchants decided to create a classification system for an upcoming trade fair, and simply based it upon prevalent pricing of the day. The result was a six-tier system of first growths (Grand Cru, or the best), second growths, third growths, fourth growths, fifth growths, and all the other wineries.

Today, there are 20,000 wine labels in Bordeaux and the 1855 Classification names just 61 of them, all along the left bank of the Gironde River. The areas not included far outstrip those along the left bank, such as Pomerol and St.-Emilion and other sites along the right bank.

Some of the important regions left out of the 1855 Classification have set up their own method: **St.-Emilion** has the most active and exacting classification. Created in

The French Label

French label laws are models for the rest of the world. They are based upon the idea that the more specific the label, the more likely that the wine is of pedigree. Thus AOC (Appellation d'Origine Côntrolée) Bordeaux is good, AOC Haut-Médoc is better, and AOC Pauillac is theoretically the best, which is generally true.

The label categories are:

VIN DE TABLE (TABLE WINE): This is not allowed to state a vintage or region of origin.

VIN DE PAYS (COUNTRY WINE): Describes massive areas such as the Pays d'Oc, which is over 100,000 acres.

VDQS OR VIN DÉLIMITÉ DE QUALITÉ SUPÉRIEURE (DELIMITED WINE OF SUPERIOR QUALITY): A holding place for wines aspiring to be AOC but not yet proven.

AOC OR APPELLATION D'ORIGINE CÔNTROLÉE (LABELED FROM A CONTROLLED ORIGIN): There are 450 AOCs accounting for about one-third of all French wine. They are the top third.

OPPOSITE, TOP: Cos d'Estournel is another "super-second," hailing from long-lived St.-Estéphe. OPPOSITE, MIDDLE: Château Lafite-Rothschild is one of the greatest estates in Bordeaux and takes a few decades to age properly. OPPOSITE, BOTTOM: Before 1987, Château Haut-Brion was labeled as Appellation Graves Côntrolée. Since then the estate is labeled as Appellation Pessac-Léognan Côntrolée, as are most of the rest of the great estates of the area.

Satellites

The satellite appellations of St.-Emilion—St.-Georges, St.-Emilion, Lussac St.-Emilion, Montagne St.-Emilion, and Puisseguin St.-Emilion—exemplify a simple, soft style, but can be great values. Pomerol also has satellites that are worthy of exploration: Canon-Fronsac, Fronsac, Lalande-de-Pomerol, and Côtes de Bourg. But Pomerol's neighbors have yet to enjoy the inflation of wine costs here. Lalande-de-Pomerol is probably as trustworthy as any St.-Emilion satellite but costs less.

1955, it was revised in 1969, 1985, and 1996. That list combines Grand Cru (over two hundred highly regarded estates), Grand Cru Classé (a select group of more than forty) and Premier Grand Cru Classé (varying between fourteen and fifteen of the very best estates).

Although there are more generals than soldiers, as others have noted, St.-Emilion never deserved to be ignored in the 1855 Classification.

St.-Emilion is usually divided into rough regions of the Côtes (or limestone and clay hills) of St.-Emilion and the Graves (or gravelly plains) though there are other, unnamed areas. The wines of these two best-known regions seemed designed to drink well young, but also age surprisingly well. Indeed, Cheval Blanc is the best available evidence that Cabernet Franc (usually 55 percent of this wine) can age and, starting in the 1990s, St.-Emilion began to offer tiny estates of impeccable quality. In this they have followed in Pomerol's footsteps.

THE RIGHT BANK'S BANK

The most valuable region of all, **Pomerol**, has never been included in any system. But in the nineteenth century, Pomerol was a place of wild vines and no order, and even today it's a relatively small and rustic place with the world's most valuable vineyard real estate. In the 1855 Classification, Pomerol didn't merit a mention. Indeed, it was not until the late 1920s that Bordeaux's most expensive wine, Château Pétrus, became an international star. Its fame had grown throughout the late 1800s, but only locally.

Pomerol's wines are very expensive, largely because the wineries produce a fraction of that released by the well-known estates of the Médoc. There the typical release is twenty or thirty thousand cases. In Pomerol, the largest estate (De Sales) offers less than twenty thousand cases. The rest average about two thousand cases—and if they demand more money, they also make less.

Nowadays, the amazing prices achieved by Pétrus, mirrored by le Pin, l'Eglise-Clinet, l'Evangile, and Lafleur among others, have become so horrifyingly expensive that they are no longer worth recommending, as much as I have enjoyed the few bottles I've been lucky enough to taste.

BORDEAUX GEOGRAPHY

After two-hundred-mile tours through the French countryside, the rivers Garonne and Dordogne gather up into the river Gironde, just past the village of Cantenac. From stem to stern, the Gironde is ninety miles of perfect harbor. It's a natural port and commercial hub.

To our purposes, it's a natural vineyard. Bordeaux is far enough north that it ought to be cold and unlikely to ripen as many grapes as it does. The two rivers meeting the one big river create a moderating effect upon the season—lengthening it in most cases and making the vintages more consistent than otherwise.

The **Médoc** is the name used to describe the vineyards along the left bank of the river Gironde, comprised of a ribbon of wineries over forty miles long and only a couple of miles wide. The wineries remain close to the river for best exposure and drainage, and proximity to the water ensures moderate temperatures, relative to the northerly latitude.

The Médoc region contains the most famous chateaux of Bordeaux within six communes, or French regions: Margaux, St.-Julien, Pauillac, St.-Estèphe, Listrac, and Moulis. Collectively these communes are known as **Haut-Médoc** and any estate upriver from St.-Seurin-de-Cadourne (near the north end of St.-Estèphe) is entitled to the appellation Haut-Médoc. Châteaux farther downriver along the Gironde use the appellation Médoc.

The communes: **Margaux** wines, as a consequence of high percentages of Cabernet Sauvignon, are harder to enjoy in their youth. **Moulis** and **Listrac**, two small communes to the north and west of Margaux, hold good wineries, but in the 1855 Classification, their wineries were left out. **St.-Julien** acts as a blend of all that is best on the left bank. Soils hold both gravel and clay, as if blending Margaux and St.-Estèphe. The wines are fleshy and perfumed like Margaux, and as rich and long-lived as Pauillac. Because the commune holds no first-growths among its ranks, the prices are fairly reasonable, for Bordeaux. **Pauillac** contains three of the five First Growths and therefore demands high prices, even for its lowliest wines. In truth, these wines tend to live the longest of any Bordeaux, as they're grown on deeper gravel soils and are usually composed with greater amounts of Cabernet Sauvignon. There are enormous differences in quality. **St.-Estèphe** has always had a reputation for hardness. But in the last twenty years, Merlot plantations have grown by over 30 percent, and the wines have become softer. The soils there are poorer, but also wetter, so the favored sites can make very special wine and the rest make so-so wine. Based upon the wines available in the American marketplace, however, St.-Estèphe is a great bargain.

Sauternes and **Barsac** contain France's best values of the last twenty years and the prices are still very fair. The Sauternes flagship, d'Yquem, is one of the few expensive wines in the world that is worth every penny, regardless of the vintage.

Dessert wines such as these live a long time. High sugar content and the high acidity that ought to go along with it, make

for stalwart wine. The dessert wines of Bordeaux are also high in alcohol, and in the right vintages, rich with the apricot and honey flavors of botrytis. Though this "noble rot" (see *Botrytis cinerea* in Glossary) doesn't occur in every vintage, its presence defines the character of Sauternes and Barsac.

The nearby rivers Cérons and Garonne allow the flow of moist air on perfect fall nights, infiltrating grape bunches with moisture. The moisture provides a site for botrytis to grow, and the grapes are desiccated by the rot. The particular conditions of this part of Bordeaux intensify the sugars in the grapes and add unique flavors.

Sauternes and Barsac are the most able dessert wine regions but other nearby, lesser-known spots on the Garonne River—Cérons, Cadillac, Loupiac, and St.-Croix du Mont—can be silly values in a great vintage, as in you're silly to ignore them.

A SHALLOW GRAVES

The **Graves** region is enormous but has been recently divided into two. The **Pessac-Léognan** vineyards are, without question, the best. None of the top twenty of Graves is outside the area. But Pessac-Léognan's abandonment of the rest of Graves is a bit like disavowing a redneck past. And, more important, at least thirty excellent wineries ply their trade in the rest of the Graves region and should not be ignored.

But the great white wines from Bordeaux are almost all from Pessac-Léognan. The wines were of uneven quality until the late 1980s but since then the best wines have been aromatic, fleshy, rich, and long of flavor and life.

SOUTHWEST FRANCE

Down south, there are myriad wines, reflecting the region's ancient history as a producer of dry white wine, sweet white wine, rosé, soft red wine, and rich reds. In some ways, Bordeaux never really stops. Instead, to the east at **Monbazillac** (great, cheap dessert wines) and at **Bergerac** (always great bargains), and to the south are some of France's most historical, but unknown, vineyards including Madiran, Cahors, Tursan, and Gaillac.

Most of these regions will remain unknown even though each contains at least one example of France's most exciting new wines. These producers will not starve, as other countries become aware of them; rather, they are excellent evidence that even the Old World of wine has not yet ceased exploding.

THE RHÔNE VALLEY

The long Rhône Valley represents France's most ancient wine land, yet it is the place of the most fervent change. As a microcosm of the rest of France's south, the change is reflected by new vineyards, new varietals, and, most important, a new sense of quality as a guiding principle.

Perhaps even more essential, the path to quality leads, apparently, to myriad destinations. As the Rhône Valley's change creeps forward, the quality producers contrast more today than five years ago. And the distinctions that exist are less about gradations of quality than differentiation of style. This point alone makes the Rhône Valley the most rewarding red-wine area in France. Why? It's safe, even recommended, to experiment.

OPPOSITE: Hermitage is so steep that helicopters are the best method for spraying vineyards.

92

The Rhône Valley physically is three places; wine-wise, it's two. It can be roughly separated into the north, the center, and the south. In the north and center, the only red grape is Syrah and there are only three white grapes: Roussanne, Marsanne, and Viognier. In the south, there are fourteen legal red grapes and nine white grapes.

The moral of this story is that, in the north and center, wines are composed of at most two grapes and usually one grape. In the south, almost everything is a complex stew of every grape possible. The Rhône Valley exemplifies the greatest single decision a winemaker must make: Shall I stick to one grape, in the belief that this grape has great character and that it expresses the flavors of my area? Or do I seek complexity by trying to harmonize as many different grapes as I can logistically grow?

But the moral runs deeper. There is a school of thought, championed by many but well expressed by Bonny Doon's Randall Grahm, among others, that climate should determine the answer to this dilemma.

Cooler climates, as partially expressed in the north and center vineyards of the Rhône, can exhibit some complexity and character within the confines of one grape. Warmer climates tend to express fewer differentiated flavors and aromas in a single variety; therefore, a skillful wine maker needs more than one grape to create interesting wine.

The north is tidy and very small, from a vineyard standpoint. The steep hills along the Rhône River allow for a limited amount of vineyard, all of which is very well placed. There is almost no Côtes du Rhône produced up north because vineyards are either great or very good, or planted to something other than grapes.

Côte Rôtie, the "roasted slope," is one of the single greatest wine hills on the planet, but it covers only 345 acres and produces only 35,000 or so cases. The Syrah grown there makes for very long-lived and chocolate-tinged wines. From the Rhône's next great hill, **Hermitage**, the wines are tougher even while they are more floral. The next hill of Syrah is the truly precipitous **Cornas** (though Côte Rôtie and Hermitage have some very scary precipices, too), and the wines are lush fruit and pure black pepper.

Best of all, the three are different and equal in every way. Despite this, Cornas should probably be consumed first because it is thicker and richer in its youth and exemplifies the great virtue of Syrah. Whether one year old or twenty, great Syrah is seemingly ready to drink. Try that with your Cabernet!

About a quarter of the wine made in Hermitage is white, usually composed of Marsanne with a dose of Roussanne. This wine is the red's opposite; sometimes it tastes as though you should wait longer to drink it, and other times it seems too late. The good news is that the wine lives for ten to twenty years, so you probably should wait.

Just south of Côte Rôtie is **Condrieu**, planted with Viognier, which nearly disappeared forty years ago. French restaurateurs discovered the rose-petal and orange-slice flavors and aromas of the most expensive wine here, Château-Grillet. Initially only Grillet benefited from the media attention; then the rest of Condrieu was discovered.

Today, Viognier is grown throughout southern France and from Mendocino to Santa Barbara in California. Its notorious growing problems don't show up in warmer sites.

Two other red wine areas may be, in the hands of a serious grower, very good to great. But only a few producers in **Crozes-Hermitage** and **St.-Joseph** are ready to prove that certain spots in these vast vineyard areas can make Syrah as good as any other.

The southern Rhône Valley is a distinctly Mediterranean place: hot, arid, fragrant, and insanely sunny. Vines don't have to struggle here; quite the opposite. And though I don't believe in the shibboleth that vines must "struggle" to be great, the wines here need something and are almost always best when created from a multiplicity of grapes.

Though this is a vast, stony, and windswept valley of vines, one small area called **Châteauneuf-du-Pape** is the moral conscience of the region. The yields here are among the lowest in France, and are enforced by law. In fact, the French wine labeling law was born here in 1926, when Baron Leroy helped protect the region by proscribing a commitment to quality. This area might provide the single greatest value in French wine, regardless of the fact that prices have doubled here in the last five to eight years.

The warm, stony soils of Châteauneuf-du-Pape. These stones can lengthen the ripening cycle by radiating heat beyond sunset.

The Côtes du Rhône are vast swales and hillside pockets of vineyards. Bottlings from vineyards around the towns of **Gigondas**, **Sablet**, **Rasteau**, **Vacqueyras**, **Lirac**, and **Cairanne** (which will be labeled with those names) represent the best of the Côtes du Rhône in degrees from delicious to intense.

The world's best rosé is grown here as well. **Tavel** is a blend of Grenache and Cinsaut and it's been the most worthy model for dry rosé wine. Yet New Worlders intent on aping the style invariably remember the Grenache and forget the Cinsaut.

One of the world's best fortified wines is grown here. **Muscat de Beaumes-de-Venise** and its little cousin, **Rasteau**, have the honey and flower flavors of the Muscat grape with great fruit intensity that allows the wines to go with a lot of desserts.

PROVENCE TO THE LANGUEDOC/ROUSSILLON

The **Provence** region is not too different from the southern Rhône, though the wines are often less interesting and a bit more expensive.

A handful of appellations near the coast do special work. Indeed, it could be trimmed down to a few wineries. **Coteaux d'Aix-en-Provence** has its Domaine Trevallon (a Cabernet/Syrah blend of impeccable character), **Palette** has Château Simone (good red, but fascinating white and rosé) and **Bandol** has Domaine Tempier. Tempier is a very special case. The owners rescued the Mourvèdre grape from extinction in the 1950s, and from there it was returned to its home in Châteauneuf-du-Pape by the owners of Beaucastel.

In the middle of the mediocre place called the **Midi**, one estate changed everything in the early 1980s. Winery Mas de Daumas planted Rhône and Bordeaux grapes in the middle of this cheap wine factory of France. Within a few years, both Michael Broadbent and Hugh Johnson, perhaps the world's best wine writers, had called Mas (its diminutive title) the greatest wine value in the world.

Imitation followed fame. Mondavi has purchased a vineyard virtually next door. The rest of the Languedoc-Roussillon, as the wider region is called, was already producing good to very good wines. Today, business is great, but you can still buy an excellent bottle from this region for ten dollars or so.

LOIRE VALLEY—THE GARDEN STATE

The **Loire Valley** is one of the most beautiful places in a country known for beautiful places. Lush with flowers, orchards, and castles, the Loire is adept at virtually every style of wine made in France. From ultra-light and dry white (Muscadet) to rich, full-bodied, and earthy red (Chinon) and the creamy sparkler (Saumur), the Loire has a complete arsenal. This and the beauty of the land have assured its place among northern European drinkers, if no others.

Muscadet can have searing acidity and a petillant sparkle when labeled Muscadet sur lie (meaning "aged on the yeast"). This wine really enjoys mussels or clams.

Coteaux du Layon, as the name implies, covers hills and valleys around the river Layon, a tributary of the Loire River. These vineyards produce remarkable wines from a very unremarkable grape, at least it is in every other place on earth. The Chenin Blanc grape, called Pineau de la Loire here, is complex and long-lived when grown in these schistose soils.

Though Coteaux du Layon and its barely better relation Coteaux du Layon Villages veer from decent to fabulous, two smaller vineyards are much more worthy of the experimental dollar. **Bonnezeaux** and **Quarts de Chaume** are two Grands Crus that are invariably sweet, brilliant, and great values.

On the north side of the Loire River, one of the great white wine appellations of the wine world, **Savennières**, is rooted in the same slate-rich soils but often has greater ripeness. It's sold as sweet, semisweet, or desert-storm dry, and is exciting in any of these forms.

Most **Saumur** wine is Chenin Blanc and is the sparkling kind. They are decent values, but excellent still Chenin grows to the north and east as well. **Jasnières** is a lesser-known appellation but trustworthy. **Montlouis** is on the south side of the river Loire and produces wines of good value. **Vouvray**, in the **Touraine** region, offers some of Chenin's greatest wines. And to the east, **Chinon, Bourgueil,** or **St.-Nicholas-de-Bourgueil** are based upon Cabernet Franc and can be excellent.

Cheverny is east of Tours along the river; from here on, the whites are all Sauvignon Blanc. The most famous appellations are **Sancerre** and **Pouilly-Fumé**, which have, until New Zealand's entry onto the scene, set the pace for solo Sauvignon Blanc. And though little here ages beyond eight years or so, the first seven can be lovely stuff. The classic wine-writer's description, "cat's pee on a gooseberry bush," implies that we spend our free time engaged in activities I can't recommend. Not that I don't like cats.

My favorite descriptors, I must admit, scarcely sound better. With young, fresh Sauvignon Blanc from these two

Sancerre and Pouilly-Fumé can be cool and misty, befitting their proximity to the Atlantic Ocean.

places, or nearby **Reuilly**, **Quincy**, or **Menetou-Salon**, I get orange and lime flavors with some leafiness or vegetables. In the best versions, I feel that there's a touch of cassis and, with a bit of age, an aroma of sweaty socks appears. And I like it (not that I spend time smelling socks).

ALSACE

Alsace has been pulled back and forth across an ever-shifting Franco-German border like a mouse between two cats. It's been a place of transition in myriad ways; the last outpost between Germania and western Europe, a hiding place for Jews in the fifteenth and sixteenth centuries, and even a combination of old wealth and peasantry—in other words, the middle class.

The defining character, for the vineyards, is the presence of the Vosges Mountains. The rain shadow effect allows for long, slow ripening of the grapes, and protects them from harvest rains. As a result the grapes, many of them Germanic in origin, reach much higher sugars (and consequently higher alcohols) than their German counterparts.

And so, while great Riesling is typically 9 percent alcohol or less in the Mosel region of Germany, here it can be 13 percent or higher. The late harvest wines, called *vendange tardive*, are often vinified dry and rich, to even higher percentages. It's as though they wanted to make German wines into white Burgundy.

Labels usually reflect only the name of the grape, not the region or vineyard. But a group of fifty-one vineyards are considered to be Grand Crus, and those vineyards will almost always appear on the label. Again, the grape is the main feature and only Riesling, Muscat, Pinot Gris, and Gewürztraminer are allowed to be labeled as Grand Cru.

This is not to suggest that sweet wines are eschewed here. SGNs (Selection de Grains Nobles) are very expensive and sought-after—they are wines made in a Beerenauslese style—from individually picked, sweet berries. The lesser grapes, Sylvaner, Chasselas, Auxerrois, Klevner and Pinot Blanc (the last three seem to be different versions of the same grape), are less respected because, for one, they don't age well. But Pinot Blanc, in particular, is delightful young and nicely indicative of the rich pear-and-crisp-apple flavors of many of Alsace's best wines.

BURGUNDY

No region epitomizes the idea of wine's sense of place as much as Burgundy. New World vintners scoff foolishly at the concept but Burgundy is proof of place. The ten feet or so separating Nuits-St.-Georges from Vosne-Romanée is instructive. Even when the wines are made in exactly the same manner, they are decidedly different. Nuits-St.-Georges is plummy, upfront, and fruity, almost Californian. Vosne-Romanée is a classic, elegant Burgundy, subtle and long.

Though some of the earth at the north end of Nuits-St.-Georges contains limestone in greater ratios than most of the appellation, the soils are usually clay-rich and the wines are fatter. The limestone-rich soils of Vosne-Romanée make for leaner and longer-lived wines.

But without question terroir is far less important than the producer. The worst Vosne-Romanée is flaccid; the best Nuits-St.-Georges can be one of Burgundy's best. As any knowledgeable wine lover knows, regardless of the region, a great producer in a so-so place, even in a so-so vintage, is far more trustworthy than a lousy producer in a great place. So, though we should concentrate on vineyards in this region of microappellations, it's imperative to shop for the producer, not the appellation.

BURGUNDY—FROM NORTH TO SOUTH

Chablis marks the northern boundary of Burgundy, but a few hundred years ago some of the eastern Loire Valley vineyards were included. Chablis is, in fact, north of a number of Loire vineyards, and was closer to the all-important Parisian market. The nineteenth-century success of the region was based upon the making of cheap carafe wine for the capital. Today, cheap wine can be made cheaper in other places.

Chablis's Grand Cru Vineyards

They include: Blanchots, Bougros, les Clos, Grenouilles, les Preuses, Valmur, and Vaudésir.

But the vineyards planted today represent a unique and beautiful expression of Chardonnay. This most northerly, coldest place for making still Chardonnay brings flavors of decidedly untropical fruit. The smell and flavor of wet river stones is the most apt descriptor for me, though others talk of flint and smokiness.

Perhaps in recognition of this unique character, few producers in Chablis use oak barrels for anything other than old containers. With barrel spiciness not a factor, the stone fruits and earth flavors can show and, with the natural acidity of these cold-climate wines, they live as long or longer than any other Chardonnay-based wine. For me, there is nothing as delightful as ten- or fifteen-year-old Grand Cru Chablis.

Côte d'Or, Burgundy's "golden slope," as it is often mistranslated, owes its pretty name to the wind that blows from the east, the "orient." The slope might as well be golden, however, since it creates some of the world's most expensive wines from some of the world's most expensive real estate.

But along the **Côte-de-Nuits** red wine prevails, as the name suggests. These are the vineyard regions: **Marsannay** is mostly Marsannay Rosé, which can be light but charming. **Fixin** is, at best, a good value. **Gevrey-Chambertin** may not be the largest appellation in Burgundy, but it has nine Grands Crus, the most of any village. Though some wine writers complain about a lack of consistency in quality or style here, that complaint could be leveled at any appellation in Burgundy. Instead, I would argue that as long as you choose wines by producer, your money is safe here. Importantly, there are Premier Cru bottlings that can outperform Grand Cru, especially Clos St.-Jacques, les Cazetiers, Combe aux Moines, les Combottes, and Lavaux St.-Jacques.

In **Morey-St.-Denis**, richness is evident but elegance seems to win out over it, at least among the best producers. The Premier Crus worth pursuing include la Bussière, les Monts Luisants, Clos des Ormes, and les Charmes. The Grands Crus **Clos St.-Denis, Clos des Lambrays, Clos de Tart** (except in the 1960s and '70s) and **Clos de la Roche** can be fairly priced as well, in that they are expensive but can equal any wine on the planet.

The other Grand Cru here is **Bonnes-Mares,** but its vines cover more territory in **Chambolle-Musigny** than in Morey-St.-Denis. Regardless of the parcel in which it is grown, the wines here are extravagant and tannic.

Chambolle-Musigny combines beautiful silkiness with dismaying power; it has an intriguing floral note. **Le Musigny,** the other Grand Cru here, perfectly exemplifies this combination, and it can live for decades.

Here, too, the Premiers Crus can be fascinating: les Amoureuses, les Baudes, les Charmes, les Cras, and les Sentiers absolutely shine. Unfortunately, the same cannot be said of the Premier Cru of **Vougeot**. While the great producers offer pretty wines from les Cras and Clos de la Perrière, the rest are usually not very compelling. In fact, the **Clos de Vougeot**, that Grand Cru walled vineyard of yore, is filled with uninspiring wine. But there are many excellent wines, not all of them clustered at the top of the hill, as books usually suggest. Instead, quality is up to the producer.

Vosne-Romanée is much more predictable. Some wines can be unworthy of their prices. The rest of the wines here are very good, in the main, but tend to be very expensive. So pre-

La Tâche, near Vosne-Romanée and Echézeaux, is one of the greatest vineyards in the world.

LA

dictability has its price, and the Premiers Crus (Clos des Réas, les Malconsorts, les Chaumes, les Cros Paranthoux, les Beaumonts, les Suchots) are both good and pricey.

And among the Grands Crus, the wines are often superlative, but the costs are too. **Les Echézeaux** and **les Grands Echézeaux** are expensive, make no mistake, but most of them are worth it, if you burn money for warmth; so too, three of the four monopoles (see Glossary), **Bouchard's** la **Romanée**, **DRC's la Tâche**, and **Romanée-Conti**. In addition, **Richebourg** and **Romanée-St.-Vivant** are just a few steps behind in superb quality and longevity. Only the other monopole, la **Grand Rue**, is a Grand Cru waiting to prove its worth.

ACHE

The Côte de Nuits ends at **Nuits-St.-Georges** and, though the wines can taste rather different from Vosne-Romanée, these are wines that are often excellent values and, in their middle years (eight to twelve years old), can be exceptional. Certainly, all the Premiers Crus can show excellence in the right hands and vintage, and proximity to Vosne-Romanée connotes wines with some of the same lovely elegance. In the Côte de Nuits some delicious white wines exist as well.

The appellations of **Haues-Côtes de Nuits**, **Hautes-Côtes de Beaune**, **Côte de Nuits-Villages**, and **Côte de Beaune-Villages** contain inexpensive wines that can show nice character, although they are invariably light and short-lived.

CÔTE DE BEAUNE

The Côte de Beaune is unquestionably the region of the world's greatest Chardonnays, but there are a number of truly great Pinot Noirs made here as well. And because the fame resides in the whites, the reds often represent good to great value.

The cohabitation of red and white begins at the north end of the region. Just above the town of Pernand-Vergelesses rises the great but huge Chardonnay vineyard of **Corton-Charlemagne**, planted with that grape, we are told, so Charlemagne's beard would not be stained by red wine. (It's a questionable tale since Chardonnay has been on this hill for perhaps less than two hundred years).

Corton Grand Cru is a far more mixed message for buyers when red than when white. Let the buyer beware of the producer, as always, but even good producers often stumble here.

Savigny-lès-Beaune and the Premiers Crus can be beautiful (les Dominodes, les Guettes, les Lavières, les Marconnets, les Narbantons, les Serpentières, and les Vergelesses) and pleasingly affordable. On either side of the highway is **Chorey-lès-Beaune**, which is more Chorey than Beaune, but can make lovely Pinot Noirs at very good prices.

Beaune is a big and ancient town (40 B.C.) and the vineyards nearby have similar pedigrees. Yet the Premier Crus are good values, perhaps because there is no Grand Cru attached to the town. Those crus to the north in limestone soils (les Bressandes, Clos du Roi, and les Marconnets), in the gravelly areas (Grèves and Teurons), and in sandy spots (les Clos des Mouches, les Sizies, and les Vignes Franches) are very different but share lovely character and longevity.

Pommard represents great red wine vineyards with wines that are long and rather hard, yet cost far less than the best from elsewhere. And the Premiers Crus (les Charmots, les Epenots, les Fremiers, les Jarolières, les Pezerolles, and les Rugiens) are fascinating at twenty years old and over.

The 1855 Classification created a system which respected the economic realities of creating and selling wine. The top growths deservedly received more money for their wines at that time and most producers continued to make the sacrifices necessary to continue to receive those high dollars. Most but not all.

The system had something of a self-fulfilling prophesy in it. By receiving more money, the top growths could afford to make top wine. Châteaux, which have made great wine, have not been compensated by being placed higher up on the classification ladder. Only one change has occurred: Mouton-Rothschild was moved from a Second Growth to a First Growth in 1973.

Indeed, if a First Growth buys a vineyard from a Fifth Growth, the wine from that vineyard automatically becomes First Growth. But, unfairly, should the First Growth estate sell the vineyard back to the Fifth Growth, it again becomes a Fifth Growth vineyard.

THE FIRST GROWTHS

Lafite-Rothschild is odd, aromatic, and even light in youth and only begins to show its potential at the end of a couple of decades. Latour is powerful from the beginning and powerful to the end, after decades. Mouton-Rothschild is fleshy and showy and, though other changes to the classification are strongly justified, only one change has occurred and Mouton was the most deserving. Throughout the entirety of the twentieth century, it has made lovely, luscious wine.

These first three are in Pauillac; the other two are Haut-Brion in Graves and Margaux in the commune of Margaux. Haut-Brion is soft and fleshy and some doubt its staying power; I disagree. Margaux is the epitome of its commune—floral, lush, and long-lived.

THE SUPER-SECONDS

There were fourteen Second Growths in the 1855 Classification and seven or eight of those make wines consistently better than the rest. Indeed, sometimes these wines are more impressive than First Growths.

Montrose and Cos d'Estournel in St.-Estèphe deserve this reputation, as does Leoville les Cases in Pauillac. Though Brane-Cantenac and Ducru-Beaucaillou are inconsistent members of the metaphorical club, the two Pichons—Pichon-Lalande and Pichon-Baron—are now charter members though the Baron only joined after the brilliant 1989 bottling.

Volnay is very close to my heart but, after all, Burgundy is meaningless unless you become irrational about it. I am fascinated by how Volnay's thick, juicy black fruits allied with acidity offers elegance as well as aging. The Premiers Crus Bousse d'Or, les Caillerets, les Champans, Clos-des-Chênes, Clos des Ducs, les Fremiets, les Pitures, and les Taillepieds can all offer amazing wine.

Barely around the corner from Volnay, **Monthelie** continues to offer more excellent value, especially from les Champs Fuillot, Meix Bataille, and Sur la Velle. However, few great producers are at work here.

In **Meursault,** white wine is king. The Premiers Crus can be brilliant and nearly as good as any Grand Cru. Look for Blagny, les Charmes, les Cras, les Genevrières, les Gouttes d'Or, les Perrières, les Poruzots, and Sous la Bois.

Puligny-Montrachet and **Chassagne-Montrachet** are named for the overarching vineyard above them, le **Montrachet.** This rather monochromatic hill faces due southeast, with the other Grand Crus nestled around: **Chevalier-Montrachet** is above, **Bâtard-Montrachet** is below, and **Bienvenues-Bâtard-Montrachet** is next to the "bastard" ("Bâtard").

A tiny slice of the hill to the west of Batard is **Criots-Bâtard-Montrachet.** In the right hands, any of these vineyards could make brilliant wine, but Le Montrachet and, to an infinitesimally lesser degree, Chevalier-Montrachet are special. Chevalier is delicate, even evanescent. le Montrachet is so rich and poised, it's like a three-hundred-pound ballet dancer *en pointe.* Ten to twenty years of aging is the norm for these wines. Nearby, the lowlier vineyards **St.-Romain** and **St.-Aubin** offer trustworthy white wine.

At the south end of the Côte de Beaune, there is a tasty and well-priced appellation called **Santenay,** with notable Premiers Crus of Beauregard, la Comme, Clos de Tavannes, les Gravières, and Maladière. There is also an obscure appellation called les **Maranges,** which formerly was bottled as Côte de Beaune-Villages.

The **Côtes Chalonnaises** contains some of Burgundy's best values in white wine and occasionally in red—**Bouzeron:** very pretty reds; **Rully:** very tasty reds and whites; **Mercurey:** good whites and some impeccable reds; **Givry:** very good reds; **Montagny:** whites only.

The **Mâconnais** has been much more successful at telling its story worldwide than the other affordable white-wine regions. This must be due to consistency as well as size, in that Mâconnais's production dwarfs any of the other regions.

The best wines come from the south, near the towns of **Pouilly** and **Fuissé.** The blend of limestone and granite shows in the rocky outcrop called Solutré, hovering over the vineyards. At the base of the cliff are tens of thousands of skeletons, from animals sent stampeding over the cliff by prehistoric hunters.

Red Mâcon is forgettable (although I had a 1912 I can't forget), and so is most of the Mâcon Blanc and Mâcon Supérieur here. But the more limited appellations, **Mâcon-Viré, Viré-Clessé, Mâcon-Loché, St.-Veran, Pouilly-Loché, Pouilly-Vinzelles,** and **Pouilly-Fuissé** have at least a few top-notch producers. Besson, Bonhomme, Château de Viré, Château-Fuissé, Ferret, Guffens Heynen, Manciat Poncet, Tête, Thevenet, and Vincent are all names worth checking out.

Most people have trouble accepting that **Beaujolais** is part of Burgundy. But then most of the Beaujolais we see might as well be Beaujolais Nouveau, as light and inconsequential as it is.

The granite soils of Beaujolais make for one of the most beautiful landscapes in French winedom, but also serve to lessen a wine's acidity. For the Gamay grape, this is a great help, and the vinification methods used here duplicate that effect.

The carbonic maceration method of fermentation—placing uncrushed grapes in a closed container—increases the overt fruitiness, but also lessens the lifespan. A few iconoclasts produce their Gamay as if it were Pinot Noir, crushing and fermenting the wine in open containers. Those wines are very special and can fool more than a few Burgundy lovers.

Yet Beaujolais is perfect for the Gamay grape and there ought to be nothing wrong with a wine that tastes great for several years and then fades. The region is separated into Beaujolais (boring), Beaujolais-Villages (better), and Beaujolais Cru (best and not at all expensive). The Crus are ten in number and so you will be buying a bottle named Brouilly, Côte de Brouilly, Chénas, Chiroubles, Fleurie, Juliénas, Morgon, Moulin-à-Vent, Régnié, or St.-Amour.

G E R M A N Y

Still there's that pesky nouveau. Though Georges Duboeuf didn't invent it, he created its popularity. I certainly can't think of any other marketer ever to send me a 45rpm recording of Frenchmen regaling their newest vintage, as Duboeuf did in the 1980s. Nouveau is Beaujolais's lowest common denominator, and perhaps it's good that there's an easy place to sell the region's lesser wines.

Marketing is annoying, but it's not the enemy of wine. Before the 1950s, Beaujolais barely existed as bottled wine. It has been Nouveau's silly rise in popularity (oh, yes, it still sells) that has allowed Beaujolais producers to convert their crop to quick cash and that has made Beaujolais visible on the world market. If that helps keep producers' doors open, I am happy for it.

GERMANY AND AUSTRIA

The reputation of German wine suffers from the public's perception of sweet wine as something embarrassing, like a leisure suit hidden in a closet. Never mind that we pour sugar into our tea and our coffee, and enjoy soft drinks—it seems the sweeter the better. In wine, anything sweet is deemed to be lesser. And Germany's wines are among the world's sweetest.

It has not always been so. The first Trockenbeerenauslese (imagine something more like honey than wine) was bottled only in 1893. But it's important to know that German wine, historically, was not sweet, certainly not as sweet as the Ausleses cheaply produced by the co-ops today. Instead, the classic version of German wine, whether from the Mosel or from the Rheingau,

As in Burgundy, many of Germany's most famous vineyards were once owned by the church.

was dry or lightly sweet. This style was not only commercially successful in the nineteenth century, but the best estates were considered the equal of the best châteaux in Bordeaux.

Auction lists, as late as the 1910s, show prices for wines from the great vineyards such as Wehlener Sonnenuhr or Brauneberger Juffer Sonnenuhr that are higher than those for comparable vintages of Château Lafite and Latour. The perceived superiority of great German estate wines was based upon their amazing longevity, especially in relation to other white wines.

This longevity still surprises people today. While most white wine is unlikely to age beyond ten years, excellent German estate wines can last far longer. In a pre-refrigeration era, a white wine, especially a lighter style wine that could live for decades, was a very valuable investment.

But the end of World War II brought temporary control by the Allies, who handed massive wine stocks over to several large cooperatives. Surely, working with a handful of wealthy capitalists must have been preferable to dealing with a multitude of farmers, many with less well-hidden Nazi pasts. The outcome was a concentration of assets, wine, facilities, and cash in the hands of a few and the business of German wine has never recovered. Make no mistake, the 1950s, '60s and most of the '70s were very kind to the key German brands. These were eras in which brands, in general, ruled. We drank Mateus, Lancer's, and German wines such as Blue Nun, Piesporter Michelsberg, Moselblümchen, and Zeller Schwarz Katz, the wine with the black plastic cat hanging on the side. Pretty cool.

The great vineyards of the steeply sloping hills above the Mosel, Saar, Ruwer, or Rhein rivers are notoriously difficult and expensive to cultivate. The low prices engendered by the low-cost, flatland vineyards planted in the 1950s and '60s were disastrous. Wine producers had to either increase yields to levels deleterious to quality or focus upon these easier, low-quality sites. General low pricing prevented great producers from receiving realistic money for their hard work, and few continued to produce great wine.

Throughout the 1970s and early '80s, buyers rarely would part with fifteen dollars for great Auslese; there was plenty to be found for half that, never mind that it was from a dreadful site, composed of substandard grapes. It was labeled Auslese, therefore it must be the same, only at a lower price.

The 1971 German wine law that enshrined the words Spätlese and Auslese (among others) into the wine buying public's mind was created by and for the co-ops. It purposefully downplayed the importance of the vineyards and grapes. Instead, second-rate grapes (Segerrebe, et al.) are rated by the same standards as the great Riesling grape, which is patently absurd.

German wine sales have declined, fueled by lower prices and the success of wine coolers and other similar beverages. For those of us who believe deeply that great German estate wines are perhaps the greatest white wines in the world, this is not terrible news. Now, perhaps, the great estates may have a chance to be seen outside of the field of mediocrity.

Moreover, the 1990s were perhaps the greatest decade in the last century or two, and prices for the best wines have finally begun to rise. Still, great German estate Riesling remains the greatest wine value in the world.

As our respect catches up with the quality here, so too our understanding may encompass the difference between the delicacy of the great wines of the Mosel, Saar, and Ruwer rivers and the richness of those wines along the Rhein. The best producers of the Rheingau, Rheinhessen, and the Pfalz create balance despite the intensity of fruit that the slightly warmer conditions and richer soils

---

The German Label

German labels are intended to convey details of origin, grape, quality, and flavor, but they merely confuse these issues.

WINE CATEGORIES OF QUALITY

TAFELWEIN: table wine

LANDWEIN: similar to a French Vin de Pays and rarely used

QBA: quality wine from a specific region

QUALITÄTSWEIN MIT PRÄDIKAT, OR QMP: quality wine with special distinction

THE STYLE CATEGORIES OF QMP

KABINETT: usually dry or off-dry

SPÄTLESE: late-picked wine which can vary from off-dry to sweet

AUSLESE: wine from late-picked and/or hand-selected grapes, which can vary from somewhat sweet to very sweet

BEERENAUSLESE (BA): individually selected berries—very sweet

TROCKENBEERENAUSLESE (TBA): sweeter BA with some botrytis

EISWEIN: BA or sweeter that's been picked while frozen

bring. In the Baden and the Nahe, though comparable wines are possible, current offerings have shown less poise and oak cooperage has reared its international head.

Vineyard name and grape appear on any good quality wine, though many of the best producers are now offering an "Estate Riesling," which is a blend of wines from various vineyards. Though these are QbA wines, they can be great values. Spätlese or Auslese may appear as "trocken" wine, which indicates that the wine is not sweet and is fuller-bodied like Alsace wine.

AUSTRIA

Today, Austria is a high-priced but successful producer of the Riesling, Grüner Veltliner and Zweigelt grapes. In the United States, the critics have been more positive than the public, but the quantities are not so great that prices have been affected.

The occasional brilliant intensity of Zweigelt belies its humble origins, crossed from Limberger and an unknown grape called St.-Laurent. But it's with white wines that Austria demands room on the main stage.

Similar to Alsace's efforts with the grape, Riesling has beautiful fullness in the country's eastern wine regions, and extraordinary dessert wines are made in the Wachau. Still, Austria's most immediate contribution to the pantheon of excellence is the grape Grüner Veltliner. This most widely planted grape in Austria labored in obscurity and mediocrity until Austria's 1985 glycol scandal. After the discovery and conviction of a few producers concocting wines from dangerous chemicals (including diethylene glycol), Austrian wine sales plummeted worldwide. It was a blessing in disguise. As the demand and push for high quality became the response from the best producers there, Grüner showed a new face. Nowadays, the lovely character of white pepper, mustard seed, and rich, sweet pear is an international sensation; it's hoped that it will remain so.

FROM EASTERN EUROPE TO NORTHERN AFRICA

Wine's birthplace spans much of the Near East but has thrived throughout the Mediterranean basin. Many parts of Eastern Europe have histories as long as the more famed regions, but not as rich. Modernity has been slower to strike in most of these vineyards and wineries, and value is the best (and only) recommendation.

However, there is no reason that any of these regions should not create excellent wines aside from a lack of intent. Bulgaria can offer excellent value, though most of the best wines are not available in the United States. Even Israeli and Lebanese bottlings offer hope that excellence here, as throughout the rest of the world, is soon coming.

Only Hungary's Tokaji is world-class wine. Indeed, from the fifteenth to twentieth centuries, it was considered to be the equal of d'Yquem, Lafite-Rothschild, Pétrus, and Romanée-Conti. Exciting dessert wines are made anyplace wine is grown, but Tokaji is a wine of amazing longevity. It's based upon botrytised grapes (Hárslevelü, Furmint, and Muscat) that are separated into free-run juice and leftover grapes. Essencia is the prohibitively expensive free-run juice. In the not-so-recent past, it was fortified before bottling. Otherwise the grapes are blended with grape juice from dry wine, and the sweetness of the bottled wine is indicated by the number of "puttonyos," or containers of the botrytised grapes. Buy Tokaji by the number of puttonyos:

OPPOSITE: The cellars of Tokaji are thick with mold.

110

P O R T U G A L

"three puttonyos" indicates a wine of the same sweetness as a German Auslese, "four puttonyos" suggests a Beerenauslese, and "six puttonyos" is as sweet as a Trockenbeerenauslese.

PORTUGAL

In Portugal, wine is the victim of its own success. The Portuguese love wine, and almost 20 percent of the population derive their primary income from it, in some manner. An even greater number have some familial connection to wine and wine production. Unfortunately, Portugal has been slow to rise to the challenge of a global marketplace because the wine industry has, until now, been good enough. But the Euro is a cruel master and only so much foreign currency can be collected from the tanning Swedes, Swiss, and Brits on the Algarve coast. Wine is abundant and cheap.

If the story I have just laid out followed its logical conclusion, then I might be describing the second coming of Mateus or Lancer's. But the 1950s were the last era of the one-size-fits-all wine brand. And those candleholding bottles from the '60s never came back in the same way as lava lamps and tie-dye.

Portugal's great strength, as with Italy and Spain, is a plethora of unknown grapes and places. Although a few Portuguese grapes appear in Chapter 3, most of the table grapes here are too limited in acreage to merit inclusion. More interesting wines are produced in Portugal from blends: white Vinho Verde is a crisp, apple-tinged mix of Alavrinho, Loureiro, and at least six other grapes. To the east, in the resurgent Dão, the reds are a rich stew of grapes, much as the new region of the Alentejo is trying to create. Only Bairrada has focused upon one red grape, Baga, with limited success. But the new trend in Portuguese wine is single-variety bottlings. Wines with grape names such as Aragones, Trincadeira Preta, Alfocheiro Preto, and Encruzado sell in Portugal but are likely to have limited success elsewhere.

Portugal's most famous wine is its Port, named for the town of Oporto. Grown in the hot and arid Douro Valley, Port wine is fortified before the wine is finished fermenting, killing the yeast and retaining some natural sweetness. It exists in two styles: tawny (as in tawny-colored from long aging in barrels) and ruby (as in bottled before it has lost its color). Tawny is bottled in permutations of ten-year-old, twenty-year-old, thirty-year-old, forty-year-old, and single-year reserve (sometimes called colheita). To the Portuguese, ten- and twenty-year-old tawnies are the best and most popular expression of the region. However, it should be noted that the age stated on the label is not necessarily the age of the wine. Rather, a twenty-year-old tawny might *remind* one of a twenty-year-old wine.

Ruby Port varies from the ridiculous to the sublime, as the cheapest "ruby Port" is most often consumed by the French when it's blended with soda water. But the very best ruby Ports are called vintage Ports; these are bottled two or so years after they are produced and can age, in a good year, for many decades. Port producers will "declare" a Port as a "vintage Port" when they believe it is built for aging, and may do so as often as they like, though not many producers would "declare" more than a few times each decade.

Late-bottled vintage Port is, happily, just what it says: it is a vintage Port that was bottled late, after four to six years in the barrel. As such, it has lost most of its sediment in the barrel, is probably completely ready to drink upon release, and is a good value.

A relatively new category is single-quinta (or single vineyard) Port, which is usually produced in a year when producers don't "declare" a vintage Port. As an example, Warre produces a vintage Port, with usually half of the wine coming from the excellent Quinta da Cavadinha estate. In a nondeclared year, they will now offer a Quinta da Cavadinha–labeled wine and this can represent excellent value even though it may not age more than two decades.

Today, finally, Port producers are offering table wines from the Douro Valley that are made from the area's best grapes: Touriga Nacional, Tinta Roriz (Tempranillo), Tinta Cão, and Touriga Francesa, among others. These too are excellent values.

The precipitous vineyards in the Douro Valley contribute to the intensity of the wines there.

MADEIRA

Portugal's other great fortified wine, Madeira, is nearly unknown and that is a shame. Whereas similar situations can offer the savvy consumer a chance to save money, prices continue to rise here because the vineyards are simply disappearing.

When it comes to ageability, Madeira is without peer. The wine has been produced as a fortified wine in both dry and sweet styles for centuries and the vintage bottlings live virtually forever. The reason? Madeira's shockingly high acidity and the bizarre method of production, a method that ensures oxidation of the wine. Normally, oxidation destroys the fruit in a wine but, in this case, the piercing acidity enables the wine to survive.

Production is based upon an unusual tradition: Madeira was routinely shipped across the warm equator and, after its voyage, tasted better than before. Today, most of the wines are slowly warmed up to around 125 degrees Fahrenheit mirroring the equatorial conditions. The least expensive wines are roughly heated with pipes directly in the vats, but the most expensive are not heated at all. Instead, the best Madeiras, including the vintage wines, are placed in barrels in the producers' attics, allowing nature itself to heat the wine. And, in general, most of these wines spend their lives at temperatures lower than the artificially heated wines.

Moreover, some vintage wines spend their lives in untopped barrels—they're half empty. With any other wine, this would be suicidal, but Madeira is unlike any other wine. A bottle of vintage Madeira aged in these circumstances can live for decades, even after it is opened. Producers often recommend that a bottle be opened two to three *weeks* before drinking. Obviously, this is not normal wine.

The typical bottlings were labeled Sercial and Verdelho (dry styles), and Bual and Malmsey (sweeter styles) but this has changed since Portugal's entry into the European Community. Until then there had been a lot of wine with these names flowing from the island of Madeira; then Brussels began insisting that what was on the label actually was in the bottle. How narrow-minded! It turned out that the vast majority of the wine on Madeira was being produced from a grape called Tinta Negra Mole. This wine continues to be available, only now one sees it in bottles labeled as "medium-sweet" (like Bual), "medium-dry" (like Verdelho), "sweet reserve" (like Malmsey), or "dry reserve" (like Sercial). The wines still legally labeled with a grape name have become much more expensive.

Still, the best fifteen-year-old Madeiras cost no more than fifty dollars per bottle and they are very special wines. But nothing in the world of wine touches the longevity of vintage Madeira, and though the wines routinely cost more than a hundred dollars a bottle, they live forever, and are some of the world's greatest dessert wines.

SPAIN

Spain may be the next Italy. That, of course, sounds pejorative, but it's not. Really, it's not. Italy has the most exciting collection of unknown grapes, styles, and producers in the world. Those who know Italy see an emergent wine power.

Spain is still invisible to all but a few wine drinkers. Even the Spanish government's efforts at marketing focus upon the tried and true, that is, upon **Rioja**. Not that Rioja is unexciting—it's a hotbed of activity and produces the only proven long-lived wines—yet it represents a tiny fraction of the total output of the country. That output is vast; Spain is the third largest producer worldwide. Although the majority of the wine has been either forgettable or distilled into brandy, times are changing and Spain is discovering its great regions. It's not awaking from a slumber as in Italy, but finding, for the first time, great wines in its midst. This has happened in a few short years and Rioja at last has rivals.

Spain's premier estate, Vega Sicilia, had proven since the 1950s that it made one of the world's best wines. So why was the region **Ribera del Duero**, where it's grown, so unheralded? The main grape is Tempranillo, here called Tinto Fino or Tinto del País, and it is one of the two important red grapes throughout the country, including in Rioja. Spain's other great grape is Garnacha, known as Grenache in France.

The two grapes appear in nearly every great wine region, and in the ideal vineyards, they perform amazing feats of richness. These vineyards are often dependent upon the mountainous terrain. Spain is a vast plateau surrounded by a ring of mountains that provide a barrier, protecting against the rain in the north and wind in the west; in the south the mountains provide cooler, elevated vineyards.

OPPOSITE: The common view of Spain as hot and dry ignores reality. The wine regions are aided by ocean winds and elevated vineyards.

This theme is played out repeatedly, as elevation or air movement lengthens the growing season in the best vineyards. Places such as **Somontano** and **Calatayud** in the northeast, **Galicia** in the northwest, and even the Ribera del Duero in the middle west are defined by their elevations, and mountainous spots such as in **Priorat** are nearly unworkable due to the rugged heights. Even Cava producers (Cava is Spain's sparkling wine), and makers in Penedes are discovering elevated sites.

Rioja and its sister region **Navarra** are also defined by the mountains, primarily the Sierra Cantabria, which block the maritimes to the north. Rioja was created by the Romans and altered by the Bordelais when, as phylloxera destroyed Bordeaux vineyards, some vintners crossed the Pyrenees in search of uninfected vineyards. They unwittingly brought the bug along with them, but they also brought to the region the respect and ideas which set the scene for its currrent fame and fortune. In the 1960s and '70s, as Spain ended its isolation under Franco's rule, modernization in the wineries created a fruitier style of wine.

Still, as lovely as modern Rioja has been, a newer stage is being set. Today, wines are rarely aged for six years (or more) in older barrels, though that's a style I miss already. The international style is here now, but Tempranillo in new French and American oak (with some Garnacha, Mazuelo, and Graciano grapes blended in) still ends up tasting like great Spanish wine.

Most of the south is too hot to produce anything better than good wine but Andalucía is the site of something greater. Sherry is the third of the world's three great fortified wines (with Port and Madeira). The word *Sherry* is an Englishman's badly pronounced version of Jerez (say "hereth"), the name of the region. It's a triangular, hot, arid, and coastal plain vaguely bounded by the towns of Jerez de la Frontera, Puerto de Santa María, and Sanlúcar de Barrameda.

The most important feature of the region is the soil, which bakes to a hard crust in the summer sun, preserving the valuable moisture beneath it. The Levante wind, burning out of the east, concentrates the grapes and prevents grape disease. All these elements conspire to create the conditions for a great fortified wine.

Sherry is made in two essential styles: either it is rich, overripe, and usually sweet (*oloroso*), or it's a *fino*. Fino describes a dry, nutty Sherry created by exposure to a kind of yeast growth in the barrel called *flor* ("the flower"). It is decidedly not floral in appearance; rather the *flor* is a foam that looks like pond scum in a barrel.

Flor, like Sherry's grape, Palomino, and like so many aspects of Sherry, has its origins at Sanlúcar de Barrameda. The coastal town is influenced by the wet ocean wind, called the Potente, and that wind helps feed the flor. Producers place their barrels next to the open windows and the bodegas are near the sea.

Numerous wine books are disingenuous about the issue of the flor, stating that its growth is a mystery. That's nonsense. Barrels intended to be fino are fortified at lower levels (15 percent or so) than those intended for oloroso, which are fortified at higher levels to discourage flor's growth. Most olorosos are sweetened with grape paste or concentrated grape juice, but dry olorosos are occasionally offered and are delicious. Finos can be sweetened as well and sold as *amontillados*, though that word should be reserved for genuinely aged finos.

Sherry's lasting image is the solera, a group of wines from different vintages that are blended incrementally. Imagine a row of barrels with a little wine taken from the oldest barrel (say that it's from 1970). That barrel is then refilled by the 1971 wine, and the 1971 barrel is refilled by the 1972, and so on until you reach the newest barrel. The wine taken from the oldest barrel will have much of the flavor of the oldest wine, but will be composed of many younger wines. But, here too, the concept and the myth differ. The simple truth is that the flor requires new wine to continue to grow and the producers in Sanlúcar realized that by adding new wine to the barrel, the flor was replenished. Soleras are far more rare these days and most Sherries blend new and old wines with cooked grape juice or must.

If this seems complicated, indeed it is. The outcome for finos is tart wine with intensely nutty flavors, while those that hail from Sanlúcar (called *manzanilla*) have the rich tang of the sea air as well. Fino Amontillados may be nutty and a bit sweet, but the best are delicate and not at all sweet. Olorosos are usually sweet and walnut-flavored, and the extremely sweet versions have names such as East India or Cream Sherry. Palo Cortado is an uncommon category containing elements of oloroso and amontillado. Whereas most Sherries last for weeks after opening, fino loses its fascinating delicacy within hours of being opened and ideally should be consumed the same day.

ITALY

Italy is a slumbering giant no more and great wines are being produced in every region. Although only a tiny minority of producers are exploring the potential for greatness here, the same could be said of nearly every other country. The wine-drinking public has yet to pursue Italy's top estates with a fervor consonant with the quality.

If Italy seems confusing to wine students, it is. But if it seems as though Italian wine has no rules, it's not true. Italian wine has its rules, but in Italy rules are not really rules, they are merely suggestions. It's similar to crossing the street in Rome—don't assume that the sidewalk is only for pedestrians.

This is a country in love with politics, so although the labeling law was revised just a few years ago (in 1992), the system is one thing, reality another. DOC (Denominazione di Origine Controllata, similar to AOC) wines number nearly three hundred and most are unknown outside their regions.

Supposedly, the best are clustered together as DOCG (or D.O.C. e Garantita—we guarantee it!). The list of DOCGs represents not the best in the country, but the most politically adept. The first white wine selected for DOCG status was Albana di Romagna, and from that moment, it was obvious that the DOCG system was going to be subverted by the well placed.

But looking for the Italian government to create order amid chaos is to shout "theater" in a crowded fire. Instead the wine lovers of the world are exhibiting preferences that speak volumes, and winegrowers and makers themselves are proving repeatedly that, despite thousands of years of production, Italy is only now discovering its greatest wines and regions.

Greatness has always been available. The mountains that define Italy, running down its length like a spine, create a million pockets of perfect, moderate weather in an otherwise hot Mediterranean climate. Rather than describing Italy as having a Mediterranean climate, it should be defined as a mountainous country, so much so that some of the mountains in the south have colder vineyards than those in the Italian Alps. Previously, it has not been economically sane to pursue these lower yield areas. Now, with the world willing to pay fair prices, it is.

All Italian wine tours begin at the French border, though I'm sure if the French could put up a brick wall across the border, they would. In the north, at the Alps, in **Valle d'Aosta**, the climate is too cold and the area too small for wine to be an international product. The next region south, **Piedmont**, is one of the world's greatest.

The Po Valley is ideal for wine because, at least in Piedmont, it's not a valley at all but a series of hills, swales, and near-cliffs, with the flatlands still chilled by the wind and fog. The extreme temperature shift from day to night is mirrored in wines that range from unbelievably tannic and massive

Spain's Priorat is one of the most difficult vineyard regions to work in the world.

119

(Barolo, Barbaresco) to the light and sometimes insipid (Gavi DOC, Asti Spumanti DOCG).

Barolo (DOCG) and **Barbaresco** (DOCG) are the longest-lived red wines in Italy. They may well be the longest-lived, nonfortified wines in the world. Here, the concept of the hillside vineyard is taken to a ridiculous extreme. It's nothing but hillsides.

As in many other places in Italy and the world, there is a sea change happening here. Many producers are trading in their large old barrels for new French oak barricas (the Bordeaux barrels found from California to Australia). Yields are down for everyone interested in quality and vinification aims to capture and retain fruit character.

The other red wines of the region can be fascinating: Dolcetto is remarkable here (see Chapter 3, page 48), Barbera d'Asti and Barbera d'Alba are sometimes brilliant (see Chapter 3, page 45), and Nebbiolo, when grown outside the Barolo and Barbaresco areas, is lighter but can still be delicious. There are obscure red grapes such as Ruché, Freisa, Grignolino, and Brachetto that will hopefully acquire enough fans to become commercially viable.

The white wines of Piedmont can be extremely tasty, but will never be great like the red wines. Gavi, Cortese (Gavi), Favorita, and Arneis are lovely wines with floral and stone fruit notes but they are all short-lived.

Liguria is a place of cliffs, fishing villages, and crisp white and red wines; Rossese (a light red) is often good while Cinqueterre white is really tasty stuff.

Lombardia is, unlike Piedmont, waiting to be discovered. The grapes here are not as well known, and there are no proven international wines like Barolo. But there are tasty and crisp white wines, such as Lugana di San Benedetto and some serious reds and sparkling wines from Oltrepo Pavese and Franciacorta.

Beautiful Lake Garda influences nearly every vineyard in **Veneto**, from lighthearted Prosecco to the massive and earthy Amarone. Prosecco, the original sparkler in the famous drink, the Bellini, can represent dull wine, or it can be a delicious, crisp value.

Grapevines are nestled on every side of the lake, and include some of the most boring, overcropped of vineyards. Most **Bardolino**, **Soave**, and **Valpolicella** available in this country to-day are poor ambassadors for wines that can be utterly delicious. Soave's Garganega grape and Valpolicella's trio of Corvina, Rondinella, and Molinara offer extremely versatile wines for the table.

High-quality Valpolicella has three versions: Classico (think tart, chewy cherries), **Recioto della Valpolicella** (barely sweet, from dried and concentrated grapes), and **Amarone** (intense and rich). Amarone too is made from passito grapes (see Glossary), but all the sugars are fermented into a heady stew of around 16 percent alcohol. Amarone has longevity and, in the best examples, pure elegance!

The **Trentino-Alto Adige** region should not be labeled as one place; visit it and you'll see that it's clearly two. The plain of Trentino is not very different from Lombardia although it holds fewer possibilities of greatness. Alto Adige, on the other hand, might as well be in Austria; indeed the people here prefer to be considered Sud-Tyroleans, the people south of Tyrol. They are blond, blue-eyed, and Germanic. And many of the wines are impeccably clean, comparable only to German and Austrian wines. The white grapes Pinot Grigio, Renano (Rhine) Riesling, Chardonnay, Pinot Bianco, and Sauvignon Blanc are planted here to good effect, but unusual reds such as Lagrein (dark and aromatic), Marzemino (tart and textured), Teroldego (thick, plummy and brilliant, especially from Foradori) and Vernatsch (more tart texture) can be fascinating.

Friuli Venezia Giulia was once known for red wine, but now it produces Italy's cleanest and most consistently excellent white wines. Aside from Pinot Grigio, Sauvignon Blanc, and Chardonnay, the grapes are uncommon: Picolit (once revered for sweet whites), Ribolla Gialla (honeyed but clean), Tocai Friulano (a very tasty white, also known as Sauvignonasse, and widely grown in Chile), Verduzzo (tart white), Pignolo (aromatic reds), Refosco (earthy reds), and Schiopettino (lovely and elegant red wine). In a reversal of white winemaking elsewhere, the wines considered to be the best are most often blends of at least several grapes.

The vineyards of the Chianti Classico district receive sunny days and cool nights, increasing the flavor of tartness in the wine.

ALBANA DI ROMAGNA: The first white DOCG is pleasant and interesting at its best. It is often not at its best.

ASTI: The sparkling wines of Asti are DOCG regardless of whether they are Moscato d'Asti (very good stuff) or Asti Spumanti (usually lackluster).

BRACHETTO D'ACQUI: A pink bubbly that is good with chocolate but hardly more interesting than the other obscure reds of the region.

GAVI: Has not yet received its DOCG but is reported to be shortly awarded that status. Light and nearly inconsequential, usually, but sometimes very interesting.

GHEMME: For DOCG? How so? Ghemme's neighbor, Gattinara, barely deserves its DOCG status, but Ghemme must have slid in on Gattinara's coattails. Generally boring reds.

VERNACCIA DI SAN GIMIGNANO: It is probably deserving of this status but it still is only a pretty white wine with a bit of longevity amongst the very best.

Emilia-Romagna, unbefittingly for a region with a capitol called Bologna, is a place of great cuisine. Just as unfairly, many of the wines are forgettable; after all, this is the home of Lambrusco. The Lambrusco available here is not the sweet frizzante that Americans virtually lived on in the 1960s, but is often dry and a lot of fun for an afternoon on the piazza. But serious? No. Sangiovese is made into solid red wine here, and the nutty Albana was the first white DOCG named in Italy for no fathomable reason.

Without question, **Tuscany** is Italy's most famous countryside, producing its most famous wine, Chianti. Thirty years ago, the region was a mess but today, Tuscany produces some of the world's best red wines. As ancient as the place is, this is a relatively new development. The potential has always been there, but the will has been intermittent.

Brunello di Montalcino (DOCG), one of the greatest expressions of the Sangiovese grape (the basis for the region's reds), was created only in the mid-1800s. Brunello, named for the dusky-colored skin of this Sangiovese clone, was found to age amazingly when grown on the favored plateau of Montalcino. Biondi Santi (the creator of Brunello) was the only great producer here until the late 1960s. Today, it's the site of true excellence, at least when nature allows. Its DOCG neighbor to the east, **Vino Nobile di Montelpulciano,** has been far less successful. The great producers only number five or so, but they are proof nonetheless that it can be done.

Much of the rest of Tuscany is covered with the rubric of Chianti, and Chianti is broken into subregions (see "Chianti's Subregions," on page 125) that only begin to hint at the diversity. Classico is clearly the best region historically. Sangiovese from here, and especially from the more ancient area bounded by the towns of Gaiole, Radda, and Castallina, is remarkable and long-lived. Only Rufina can lay claim to sharing Classico's mantle of excellence. But other DOC wines, not called Chianti, also live in the hills here: Carmignano (good reds often with some Cabernet), Pomino (more serious reds and good whites), Vernaccia di San Gimignano (a DOCG of pretty whites), and Morellino di Scansano (excellent value Sangiovese).

The newest plantings are on the southern coast, especially near Bolgheri, and Bordeaux varieties are doing marvelously here. This is the likely new home for overhyped, long-lived wines, but until then the prices should be reasonable.

East of Tuscany lies **Umbria,** a hilly outpost that served as the hiding place for popes on the run during the Middle Ages. Winemaking has ancient roots here as well but, led by Lungarotti, the area is very progressive and oriented toward excellence. Orvieto (DOC), the

The caves at Regaleali in Sicily, one of the standard bearers for the area's potential greatness.

potentially boring white wine, can be delicious, especially when it has more Greccheto than Trebbiano in the grape mix.

Almost single-handedly, Lungarotti garnered DOCG status for the Sangiovese-based blend called Torgiano Riserva, while Torgiano non-riserva remains only a DOC. For once, the label was deserved. And one of Italy's newest DOCGs, Sagrantino di Montefalco, is just as deserving and shares with Torgiano Riserva the supremacy of one producer, Arnaldo Caprai. Caprai makes intense and long-lived Sagrantino and is clearly the best evidence of Sagrantino's international respect.

Across another row of the Apennines, elevated **Marches** plummets toward the Adriatic Sea. Verdicchio is the best-known wine here (see Chapter 3, page 44) and has two homes, near the sea at Castelli di Jesi and in the sheltered Matelica valley. Both can be delightful. Rosso Conero can be even more serious, based not upon Sangiovese, but by a preponderance of the Montepulciano grape, which in typical Italian fashion bears no relation to the Montepulciano of Tuscany.

Going south from here is like heading into the Ozarks of Italy. As much as northern Italians look down upon the south, these remote spots are even more ridiculed. Wine-wise, perhaps they're not wrong; two-thirds of the wines here are made by co-ops. Excellent value Montepulciano dominates southward in **Abruzzi** and in **Molise**, which is even less frequented and was considered part of Abruzzi until 1963.

On the other side of the Apennines, the bustle of Rome is at the center of **Lazio** (Latium). Until recently the only wine made here was plonk for Roman cafes, and the wines Frascati and Est!Est!!Est!!! represented the boring best. The white wines are cleaner now, and DOCs such as Cerverteí, Marino, and Aprilia, with its textured Merlot, are exciting.

Naples, to the south, is the capital of **Campania** and the home of pizza. Perhaps it's instructive that Italians most often consume pizza with beer. But, make no mistake, there are excellent wines in Campania and even more potential great wines. The Aglianico grape is successful here and throughout the southern peninsula, as are the ancient white varieties Greco di Tufo and Fiano.

The most visible producers of these excellent grapes, the Mastroberardino family, has only in the last decade received the acclaim they strongly deserve. Without Taurasi, a DOCG made from Aglianico, this grape might never have been rescued from obscurity. As well, their wonderful Vesuvio (DOC) bottlings highlight other indigenous grapes both red (Piedirosso, or red-foot, and Sciascinoso) and white (Verdeca and Coda di Volpe), though international varieties are being grown, too.

To the east in **Basilicata**, Aglianico's reign reaches literal heights on Mount Vulture, where the cold climate may necessitate a harvest as late as November. Aglianico del Vulture has several good producers.

In **Puglia** (Apulia) there is as much wine produced as in the state of California, and little of it has been exported. Less than 2 percent of the wines are DOC. But led by the late Cosimo Taurino, vineyards near the heel of the boot that is Italy began offering wines of excellent value and now offer even better wines. Salice Salentino deserves its popularity worldwide. The determination that America's Zinfandel and Puglia's Primitivo were the same grape has spurred work with it here, but nothing very interesting has happened yet.

The toe of Italy is the region of **Calabria** and colder, elevated sites are here, too, as in Basilicata and Campania. The Gaglioppo grape makes excellent Cirò (DOC), among other wines, and should the intent and the finances arrive, Calabria will exploit more sites for this and other uncommon grapes.

Sicily deserves better than its Mafioso reputation and its historically lackluster wines. And they have clearly tried. Producers such as Regaleali and Corvo proved years ago that great wine can be made here. So the better wines (which do exist, they really do) are bound to be promoted and exported soon. The trustworthy winemakers seem to get better with every vintage, though white wine remains a challenge.

Marsala (DOC) is the most unknown of the great fortified wines. Unlike the apocryphal stories regarding the invention of other fortified wines such as Port, Marsala really was invented by an Englishman. If you have never tasted real Marsala (not the stuff you cook with), consider a wine from De Bartoli, Pellegrino, or Donnafugata. The other islands to the north and east have wine histories too. On the Lipari islands, the beautifully exotic Malvasia della Lipari (DOC) makes a perfect accompaniment to crème brûlée. Moscato di Pantelleria (a DOC from Pantelleria island) can be even richer. The island of **Sardinia** is more Spanish than Italian, and belonged to Spain for a time. Grenache is lovely here (called Cannonau) and other grapes such as Carignan, Vermentino, and Malvasia betray Iberian roots.

Chianti's Subregions

Arentini, Classico, Colli Fiorentini, Colli Senesi, Colline Pisane, Montalbano, Montespertoli, and Rufina. Though they are divergent in quality and style, all of them are considered to be Chianti DOCG.

Wine and Food

the user's guide

As I explained in the Introduction, wine is in no way as popular as it could be. Why? Because people are confused as to how it's to be used. In order to understand wine's present dilemma, we need to see that wine is tasted in America far too often without food.

Don't get me wrong, I'm not telling you to stop drinking wine without food. As far as I'm concerned you should drink wine until you're happy, and as much wine as is healthy. But wine's best purpose is to accompany food. In Italy, if you've had too much to drink (which one rarely sees there), they don't say that you've had too much to drink, they say "non basta a mangiare"— in other words, you haven't had enough to eat.

We consume a great deal of wine as cocktails and not with a meal. Worse yet, those of us who evaluate wine for a living always grade the wines without food. Of course, we have to do it that way. We are scientists! We are experts! We evaluate wine in clinical settings without the distractions accompanying food. In other words, wine judges taste in exactly the opposite setting for which the wine is created. Wine is supposed to go with food.

It's not simply historical but physiological as well. *Adaptation* is the term used to describe the manner in which our brains will screen out dominant aromas, in order to smell new ones. Think of the first bite of prime rib. What could be better—it's succulent, juicy, perfect. The second bite? Excellent. The third? It's good. By the fourth bite, if the waiter asks, "How's the prime rib?" you would probably say, "It's okay, just a little overdone."

BELOW: Chocolate is tough on wine but likes Ruby Port's higher alcohol and texture. OPPOSITE: Mussels and red wine? Shellfish and red wine are not a good combination for some people, as the umami in the fish tends to make tannic wines more bitter.

Adaptation is a survival mechanism that enables people to differentiate new and important smells, even when there is something intensely smelly present. Now take food and wine. The brain tastes the food but after three bites it says been there, done that, what else you got? Enter wine, a new aroma and flavor. Now when you have a bite of food, you alternate it with the wine, then you introduce food flavor, then wine flavor, food, wine, food, wine, and then it's time for a nap.

Wine's purpose is not only to change the flavors but to clean the mouth of residual flavors. This unfortunate necessity has caused the entire wine and food debacle. Because of this, some snooty sommelier is going to criticize the wine you've ordered because "it doesn't go with your food."

First off, who cares? It doesn't have to go with one's food, it just has to go with one's guests. Second, the sommelier should not care what a patron orders. He's not drinking it. People should drink what they want, when they want, and how they want.

CHOCOLATE, LIVER, AND ONIONS

As we try to grip this issue of taste by the nose, bear in mind that there really is no such thing as consensus when it comes to flavor. Picture a big gooey chocolate cake. Sounds good, right? Well, imagine that there are a whole lot of us who don't like chocolate cake. Now, picture a pan full of sweet onions and a searing calf's liver. Some people think it's disgusting, but I think it's one of those great food smells that prove to me I'm more concerned with great flavor than with my own health.

Wine is too complicated, as explained by most of us wine writers. We've created rules and the perception of rules that hinder the most important element, relaxation.

Worst of all are our words. Tannin. Acid. Dry. Sweet. Residual Sugar. Oaky. Corky. These words convey practically nothing or, worse, have no agreed-upon meaning. The cacophony is enough to make a wine buyer cry "beer"!

Whereas there are strict definitions for these terms, using a word such as "acidity" suggests an evaluative precision that most people are incapable of perceiving. More important, those components are not what we humans taste, not in as much as we perceive flavor as a collection of aromas and tastes.

Though the perception of flavor is as muddy as it's ever been in mankind's history, let us settle the matter and seek clarity on these ancient issues. As stated in Chapter 2, the typical view is that there are four tastes: sweet, sour, salty, and bitter. I use the word typical and not historical, because the concept of four primary tastes is a late-nineteenth-century one. Prior to that time writers posited two tastes, or three, or many.

FIVE TASTES?

The first-known food-science book is a twenty-five-hundred-year-old text titled *The Yellow Emperor's Classic of Internal Medicine*. In it, five flavors were found and in my edition they were translated as sweet, sour, salty, bitter, and pungent. The translator lacked an English-language correlation for the fifth flavor and so chose "pungent" but a quick glance at twentieth-century Japanese food books revealed that the fifth flavor was believed to be something called "umami," or "delicious."

Descriptions of umami are still debated but I prefer "brothy" to any other. The foodstuffs rich in umami include shellfish, broccoli, and tomatoes, and umami's presence can be detected

Caviar has lots of umami—one of the reasons that wines with tannin are not preferred with it.

even by small infants. In virtually all testing upon humans of all ages, races, and sexes, food with umami is preferred to food without umami.

Wine clearly contains elements that taste of acid, bitterness, or sweetness. It is still debated as to whether some wines contain umami. Tim Hanni, a California educator in these matters, insists that some wines do. Research will shortly answer that question. What is more important, however, is to consider wine's impact on food and food's impact on wine, based upon these tastes.

We do not all experience the sensation of taste alike; the flavor one person tastes may not be the same as that tasted by someone else. That's why I've framed the following so-called rules of food and wine matching as merely recommendations.

1. Acidity in food can make soft wines seem flabby. High acid foods, including tomatoes and vinegars, seem most comfortable with wines of moderate of higher acidity. These include German, northern French, and Italian wines.

2. Salt buffers acidity and bitterness. That means that salty foods (such as shellfish or a strong hand on the salt shaker) can make a big, astringent red seem less so. In addition, salty foods can reduce the intensity of a low intensity wine, making it seem smaller.

Lamb is traditional with red wine, but rich or even sweet wines of any shade can go well with it.

3. Foods with umami such as shellfish, seaweed, and tomatoes can challenge wine but both salt and acidity can reduce its intensity and make the wine seem softer and fleshier. Umami tends to make tannic, bitter wines taste more bitter and, some even say, metallic.

4. When the food is sweet, as many sauces and food preparations can be, the wine must have fruity intensity so as not to seem meager and stingy next to the food. In fact, there is a simple rule that one applies to dessert and dessert wines; the wine should be as sweet or sweeter than the dessert.

Interestingly, as restaurants and bars explore the concept of spirits and food matching, one of the two rules I teach is the following: Make certain that the cocktail is a bit sweeter than the dish. The other rule: The higher the proof, the less likely that lots of people are going to like it.

And lest I leave the wrong impression, we are not yet certain how many primary tastes actually exist. Some scientists believe that we already know of more tastes (potassium chloride for instance), and there are perhaps several yet to be discovered. Others believe that the concept of primary taste is itself flawed—rather, we detect flavors in a sort of continuum, and the known tastes are simply points on a spider graph.

The insight that Tim Hanni, for one, has applied to some of these concepts leads him to recommend that dishes be balanced among all these five elements in order to be friendly to wine. So he has advised chefs to utilize salt or acidity as befits the wine being served.

Having said all this about taste, let us now recall the overarching issue of aroma. Anyone who has ever had a cold, or a child holding down his or her nose in order to force down the spinach, knows that if you can't smell, you can't taste.

Most people make up their minds as to how foods and wines go together based upon a similarity of aromas. There's nothing inherently wrong with this, just as there is nothing wrong with any preference someone has about wine. But our perception of the flavor of any drink or food is a combination of aromas, tastes, textures, and other physio-chemical sensations. Textures may include astringency (which usually accompanies bitterness); oiliness; weight (higher alcohol wines can seem heavier in the mouth, or more textured); tartness (acidity physically dries out the mouth); and bubbles, which may be light (as in frizzante) or very intense (as in young Champagne) but either way have the sensation of lightness and can dry out the mouth.

No one component of flavor is necessarily more important than the others. And the complications guaranteed by these components help explain why there is no single wine likely to please all diners with any single dish. Instead, the possibilities are nearly endless, only limited by the preferences of the drinkers and by the balance between the wine and the food. This balance bears exploring.

There are several reasons why wine is particularly well equipped to be food's foil. First, it has fairly high acidity, at least compared to beverages invented in the twentieth century. Acidity links up with moisture in the mouth, effectively drying it. This dryness helps remove the food's flavor from the mouth.

Second, the response to the dryness is to salivate, which causes the brain to request that gastric juices begin flowing in anticipation of food. Suddenly, a person feels hungry and hunger always makes food taste better, a concept tested far too often in some of the slow-service restaurants I frequent. But think of the beverages we drink before dinner: dry martinis, Champagne, dry white wine, Campari, and soda. All these make people hungry.

Third, red wine has an element called tannin that also has a scouring effect on the flavors in the mouth. Tannin is a key player in the red wine and health phenomenon; its presence usually indicates resveratrol and quercetin, compounds found to lower incidence of stroke and heart disease. Just as these compounds may help you live longer, they also enable a wine to survive a long sojourn in the cellar. As time goes on, tannin and the elements that color a wine bond into larger molecules, eventually becoming large enough to see and falling to the bottom of the bottle as sediment. The sediment's presence is a fairly flawless method of determining that a bottle is ready for consumption.

Wine exhibits other virtues with food since, as a low-alcohol drink, it aids in digestion and calms the mind during the most important meals. Eating while drinking slows the rate of drunkenness. The advantages to that are clear.

THE FOOD THAT LIGHTENS THE SPIRIT

For most of our species's history, wine has been the only safe beverage, since its alcoholic stew inhibits microbial growth. Our forefathers and mothers mixed it with water, and it made water safe. Wine made meals more nutritious and wholesome, and made life a little more pleasant.

Indeed, for most of our history wine has been food and, if it was not the most essential food, it was at least the most peaceful food. Only mother's milk is better. But that, like wine, is a very personal matter of taste.

OPPOSITE: Red wine and cheese are a popular combination. But white wines are a more consistent match, especially for tart cheeses like goat cheese.

133

The following are books I find indispensable to further wine studies.

BOOKS

Adams, Leon. *The Wines of America*. New York: McGraw-Hill, 1990.

Anderson, Burton. *Vino*. New York: Little, Brown and Company, 1980.

Anderson, Burton. *Wine Atlas of Italy*. New York: Simon and Schuster, 1990.

Asher, Gerald. *On Wine*. New York: Random House, 1982.

Beauchamp, Gary, and Linda Bartoshuk, eds. *Tasting and Smelling*. New York: Academic Press, 1997.

Benson, Jeffrey, and Alistair MacKenzie. *Sauternes*. New York: Rizzoli, 1990.

Broadbent, Michael. *The Great Vintage Wine Book*. London: Mitchell Beazley Publishers, 1992.

Clarke, Oz. *New Classic Wines*. New York: Simon & Schuster, 1991.

Coates, Clive. *Côtes d'Or*. Los Angeles: University of California Press, 1998.

Coates, Clive. *Grands Vins*. Los Angeles: University of California Press, 1995.

Coates, Clive. *The Wines of France*. San Francisco: Wine Appreciation Guild, 1990.

Cocks, Charles, and Edourard Feret. *Bordeaux and its Wines*. Bordeaux: Editions Feret, 1995.

Croft-Cooke, Rupert. *Madeira*. London: Putnam, 1961.

Duijker, Hubrecht. *The Great Wines of Burgundy*. London: Mitchell Beazley Publishers, 1983.

Duijker, Hubrecht. *Wine Atlas of Spain*. New York: Simon and Schuster, 1997.

Evans, Len. *Complete Book of Australian Wine*. Melbourne: Lansdowne Press, 1985.

Friedrich, Jacqueline. *Wine and Food Guide to the Loire*. New York: Henry Holt and Company, 1996.

Garner, Michael, and Paul Merritt. *Barolo*. San Francisco: Wine Appreciation Guild, 1990.

George, Rosemary. *Chianti*. London: Phillip Wilson Publishers, 1990.

Gregutt, Paul, et al. *Northwest Wines*. Seattle: Sasquatch Books, 1996.

Halliday, James. *Australian Wine Guide*, New York: HarperCollins, 1990.

Halliday, James, and Hugh Johnson. *The Vintner's Art*. New York: Simon and Schuster, 1992.

Huang-Ti and Ch'l-Pai, with a translation by Ilza Veith. *The Yellow Emperor's Classic of Internal Medicine*. Los Angeles: University of California Press, 1972.

Hughes, Dave. *South African Wine*. Cape Town: Struik Publishers, 1992.

Jackson, Ron. *Wine Science*. New York: Academic Press, 1997.

Jefford, Andrew. *Port*. New York: Exeter Books, 1988.

Jeffs, Julian. *Sherry*. London: Faber and Faber, 1982.

Jeffs, Julian. *The Wines of Spain*. London: Faber and Faber, 1999.

Johnson, Hugh. *Vintage: The Story of Wine*. New York: Simon and Schuster, 1989.

Johnson, Hugh, and Hubrecht Duijker. *Wine Atlas of France*. New York: Simon and Schuster, 1987.

Julyan, Brian. *Sales and Service for the Wine Professional*. New York: Cassell Publishing, 1990.

Kawamura, Yojiro and Morley Kame, eds. *Umami: A Basic Taste*. New York: Marcel Dekker, 1987.

Kramer, Matt. *Making Sense of Burgundy*. New York: William Morrow and Company, 1990.

Lynch, Kermit. *Adventures on the Wine Route*. New York: Farrar, Straus and Giroux, 1988.

Mayson, Richard. *Portugal's Wines & Winemakers*. San Francisco: Wine Appreciation Guild, 1992.

Miller, Lee. *Wine: East of the Rockies*. Lancaster, Penn.: L&H Photojournalism, 1982.

Muscatine, Doris, ed., et al. *The Book of California Wine*. Los Angeles: University of California Press, 1984.

Norman, Remington. *Rhône Renaissance*. San Francisco: Wine Appreciation Guild, 1996.

Parker, Jr., Robert M. *Bordeaux*. New York: Simon and Schuster, 1985.

Parker, Jr., Robert M. *Burgundy*. New York: Simon and Schuster, 1990.

Parker, Jr., Robert M. *The Wines of the Rhône Valley and Provence*. New York: Simon and Schuster, 1987.

Penning-Rowsell, Edmund. *The Wines of Bordeaux*. San Francisco: Wine Appreciation Guild, 1985.

Peppercorn, David. *Bordeaux*. London: Faber and Faber, 1991.

Peynaud, Emile. *Knowing and Making Wine*. New York: John Wiley and Sons, 1984.

Peynaud, Emile. *The Taste of Wine*. San Francisco: Wine Appreciation Guild, 1987.

Piggott, Stuart. *Life Beyond Liebfraumilch*. London: Sidgwick and Jackson, 1988.

Piggott, Stuart, and Hugh Johnson. *Wine Atlas of Germany*. London: Mitchell Beazley, 1995.

Pinney, Thomas. *A History of Wine in America*. Los Angeles: University of California Press, 1989.

Radford, John. *The New Spain*. London: Antique Collector's Club, 1998.

Robinson, Jancis, ed. *The Oxford Companion to Wine*. Oxford: Oxford University Press, 1994.

Robinson, Jancis. *Tasting Pleasures*. New York: Penguin Books, 1999.

Robinson, Jancis. *Vines, Grapes and Wines*. London: Mitchell Beazley Publishers, 1986.

Robinson, Jancis. *Vintage Time Charts*. London: Mitchell Beazley Publishers, 1989.

Rosengarten, David, and Joshua Wesson. *Red Wine with Fish*. New York: Simon and Schuster, 1989.

Schreiner, John. *The World of Canadian Wine*. Vancouver: Douglas and McIntyre, 1985.

Smart, Richard and Mike Robinson. *Sunlight into Wine*. Adelaide, Australia: Winetitles, 1991.

Spurrier, Stephen. *Academie du Vin Guide to French Wine*. Topsfield, Mass.: Salem House, 1986.

Steinberg, Edward. *The Making of a Great Wine*. Hopewell, N.J.: Ecco Press, 1992.

Stevenson, Tom. *Christie's Encyclopedia of Champagne and Sparkling Wines*. San Francisco: Wine Appreciation Guild, 1999.

Stevenson, Tom. *Sotheby's World Wine Encyclopedia*. London and New York: Dorling Kindersley Publishers, 1995.

Sutcliffe, Serena. *Champagne*. London: Mitchell Beazley Publishers, 1988.

Wilson, James E. *Terroir*. San Francisco: Wine Appreciation Guild, 1999.

Zoecklein, Bruce, et al. *Production Wine Analysis*. New York: Van Nostrand Reinhold, 1990.

Zraly, Kevin. *The Complete Windows on the World Wine Course*. New York: Sterling Publishing, 1985.

MAGAZINES

The Art of Eating

The California Grapevine

Decanter

The International Wine Cellar

Santé

Saveur

The Underground Wine Journal

Clive Coates, the Vine

The Wine Advocate

The Wine Spectator

Acidity: The natural grape acids that give wine its tartness and that provide the structure of white wines. High levels of acidity enable certain wines to live longer, especially Madeira and German wines.

Amabile: Describes wines that are slightly sweet from Italy, and are often the most traditional expression of those regions' wines.

Amaro: An Italian word that means "bitter," and is implicit in Amarone, the Veneto's great, slightly bitter, full, and rich wine.

Amontillado: A delicious, almond-flavored type of fino (or dry and light) sherry that has aged in barrels for long periods of time. Unfortunately most commercially available Amontillados are simply sweetened finos without the aging.

AOC: Abbreviation for Appellation d'Origine Côntrolée, indicating that a wine comes from a particular place in France and that the wine's production has been controlled by the French government.

A.P. number: German abbreviation for Amtliche Prüfnummer, indicating that the wine has been tested for authenticity and certified by the German government.

Aroma: Often described as the smell of the grapes in a wine, as separate from the bouquet that derives from the wine's time in the bottle. It is also described as the smell of the wine in total.

Aromatized wine: Describes wines, such as vermouth, which are blended or infused with herbs and plants. Most are aged but still have very high acidity and work best as aperitifs.

Autolysis: The breakdown of yeast cells in a bottle of Champagne, or quality sparkling wine, which can give a yeasty, sometimes toasty and nutty, aroma that increases as the wine sits on its yeast. Great Champagne may sit on its yeast, or lees, for five years or more.

Balance: This subjective descriptor expresses the interplay in a wine of the fruit with its structuring elements: tannin and acidity. If these elements are in "balance," no one characteristic component stands out and the wine is likely able to live for several years in this state of grace.

Wines out of balance may be impressive and rich, but are considered to be unlikely to age beyond a few more years. Though some writers such as Clive Coates are better than others at predicting longevity, the question of balance is mostly based upon subjective observations.

Barrel-fermented: White wines that have been fermented in oak barrels show spice flavors such as ginger, nutmeg, dill, coconut, allspice, black pepper, and clove, as well as greater texture and creaminess than wines aged without oak barrels.

Blanc de Blancs: White wine made from white grapes; in Champagne, this means that the wine is wholly Chardonnay.

Blanc de Noir: A white wine made from red grapes (most grape juice is clear or "white"); in Champagne, a sparkling wine made from Pinot Meunier and Pinot Noir.

Bio-dynamic agriculture: An agricultural system founded almost one hundred years ago that eschews all but the most natural and organic methods. Indeed, its sometimes arcane practices indicate a philosophy of nearly religious and mystical character.

Body: The body of a wine is chiefly the result of the alcohol in the wine; the more alcohol, the bigger the body.

Botrytis cinerea: The "noble rot," as this is often called, dessicates grapes and helps create the sweet juice that typifies Sauternes and Monbazillac, German Trockenbeerenauslese, and other great sweet wines.

Bouquet: Generally understood to be the smell a wine gains from bottle-aging.

Brix: A measurement of the sugar content in grape juice.

Brut: The standard style of sparkling wine or Champagne, with less sweetness than the style called "Extra Dry."

Carbonic Maceration: A process used primarily in Beaujolais that increases fruitiness and lowers acidity. The fermentation takes place in a closed container, and within the uncrushed grapes.

Charmat: A less-expensive method of making sparkling wine than the *méthode traditionelle* or *méthode champenoise*; here the secondary fermentation takes place in a large container, not in the bottle. This is known as "cuve close" as well.

Claret: the British term for red Bordeaux, which implies a classic, if somewhat unpretentious, example of the wine.

Clone: Each type of grapevine often has minor variations, which may be identified as clones and which may exhibit specific characteristics in specific places.

Colheita: The Portuguese word for vintage.

Corked Wine, Cork Taint: Describes a wine with an "off" aroma from TCA, (trichloro anisole), a cardboard-like smell that comes from a bad cork.

Cosecha: The Spanish word for vintage.

Cream Sherry: A sweetened oloroso sherry.

Crémant: The term for non-Champagne sparkling wines in France.

Cru: An estate (or growth) in France, usually denoting a member of a hierarchy, such as Premier Cru to Grand Cru, or first through fifth growth.

Cuve close: see *Charmat.*

Demi-sec: A sweeter style of Champagne or sparkling wine, erroneously translated as "Extra Dry" in America.

Disgorgement: The process of removing lees, or yeasts, from a Champagne bottle.

DO: The Denominación de Origen designation denotes a Spanish wine category much the same as France's AOC.

DOC: In Italy (Denomincao di Origine) and in Portugal (Denominacao de Origem Controlada), wines labeled with similar restrictions to France's AOC. Italy's DOCG (the "G" is for "Garantita") guarantees that the wine comes from twenty or so areas that sometimes deserve more respect.

DOCa: A Spanish designation similar to DO but includes the Calificada (Ca), or guaranteed to be of the best quality.

Eau de Vie: A brandy, usually not aged, made from fruit wine.

Edelzwicker: An Alsace white wine blended from lesser grapes.

Erzeugerabfüllung: A German term meaning "estate bottled," but rarely is. It has now been replaced by "Gütsabfüllung," which is more likely to be an estate-bottled wine.

Estate bottled: A term used to describe a wine grown, made, and bottled by one producer.

Fermentation: The process by which yeast converts sugar to alcohol and carbon dioxide.

Flor: A yeast scum that looks nothing like the "flower" in the name, protects a wine from air while it is developing in the barrel and imparts flavor; used to make Fino Sherry in Spain and *vin jaune* in France.

Fortified wine: A wine blended with grape spirit or brandy to achieve an alcohol content of 15 percent or more. Though the famous fortifieds are Port, Sherry, and Madeira, most wine-producing countries offer similar wines.

Frizzante: Italian term for lightly sparkling wine.

Garrafeira: A Portuguese term for reserve wine.

Grand Cru: "Great growth," a French term denoting an estate or vineyard that is deemed by the authorities to be at the top of its class. However, the term suggests different things in different places there.

Gütsabfüllung: see *Erzeugerabfüllung.*

Halbtrocken: German term for "half-dry," which is barely dry or semi-sweet.

Lees: Dead yeast cells found in the bottom of barrels and in Champagne bottles before disgorgement; their presence adds richness and toastiness.

Maderization: As wines break down in the presence of oxygen, we say that they become maderized, or similar to Madeira, which is made under oxidative conditions. The resultant flavors are nutty or applelike.

Malolactic fermentation: A secondary fermentation that is nearly universal in red wines and common in oak-aged white wines. With it, apple-flavored malic acid is converted to creamy lactic acid.

Méthode champenoise: The traditional method of Champagne production used to make high quality sparkling wines around the world. Outside of Champagne, the term is supposed to be *méthode traditionelle.*

Monopole: French term used primarily in Burgundy to describe a vineyard with only one owner, as opposed to the multiplicity of ownership typical there.

Mousseaux: An obsolete term for sparkling wine outside of Champagne; now replaced by "crémant."

Must: Term used to describe unfermented grape juice.

Oak barrel: A traditional vessel for wine used by the Romans and in wide use ever since. If the oak is new, the flavors imparted are intense; if the barrel is used several times, it has much less flavor.

Oxidation: The slow process by which a wine becomes oxygen-infused, thereby losing its flavor.

Passito: These grapes are air-dried to increase their sugar content and are usually used for dessert wines.

Phylloxera: A vine-killing louse that wreaked devastation upon the world's vines a century ago and still causes problems today. Vines must be grafted onto American rootstocks in order to withstand the louse.

Pierce's Disease: A deadly bacteria affecting vines in California and native to both the American Southwest and Southeast.

Reserva, Riserva: Term meaning greater merit and barrel-aging in wines in Spain, Portugal, Italy, Chile, and Argentina.

Reserve: As above, though in American usage the term has been overused and has no legal meaning.

Residual sugar: The amount of sugar remaining in a wine after fermentation. Most "dry" wines have less than .5 percent residual sugar, while a sweet wine may have from 1.5 to 5 percent residual sugar.

Sediment: The grains and chunks that develop in a wine container as the wine ages. Composed of tannin, coloring matter, and sometimes tartrate crystals.

Sekt: A sparkling wine from Germany; if labeled as "Deutscher Sekt," it's made from German grapes.

Solera: A system of fractional blending of different vintages used to make Sherry and other fortified wines. The concept is based upon the intermingling of older and newer vintages, which tends to enrich the younger vintages.

Spumante: Sparkling wine in Italy, dry or sweet, though the most famous (Asti Spumante) is always sweet.

Sulfur dioxide: A natural element used in wine production in trace amounts for stability since the early 1600s.

Süssreserve: Unfermented grape juice used in German wines to add sweetness.

Sweet wine: Wines with more than 1.5 percent residual sugar often are considered to be sweet, but wines with less sugar can seem sweeter dependent upon the amount of acidity. That is, a wine with 1 percent residual sugar and very low acidity (tartness), will seem sweeter than a wine with 1.5 percent sugar and very high acidity.

Tannin: The acid found in the skins, stems, and seeds of wine grapes (as well as the barrels used to age wines) that give a dusty, astringent, somewhat bitter character to wine. As the wine ages, tannin combines with coloring matter to produce sediment.

Trocken: A German term meaning dry, or very low residual sugar, wine.

Ullage: Describes the gradual reduction of the volume of a wine in bottle as it ages. Some ullage is natural, but gross ullage is likely due to mishandling of the wine or malfunction of the cork.

Varietal: A type of vine and, hence, grape and wine. Wines are either blends of varietals or labeled as a single variety. Labeling requirements of varieties vary widely: America requires 75 percent, though Oregon requires 90 percent and Missouri 85 percent; many European countries require more.

VDQS: An abbreviation for Vins Délimité Qualité Supérieure, a level below AOC.

Vin de Mutage: A term describing a fortified wine.

Vin de Pays: A French wine "from the country," a level below VDQS and AOC.

Vin de Table: The bottom of the quality pyramid in French wine labeling.

Vinifera crossing: Grape type created by crossing two varieties of native European wines. Pinotage, for example, was grown from a crossing of Pinot Noir and Cinsaut.

Vitis Labrusca: One of many native American grapevine species and, as with most other native grapes, a musky smell accompanies the wine.

Vitis Vinifera: The vine native to Eurasia which provides most of the good and all the great wines. Among the individual types are the famous names, such as Chardonnay, Merlot, Cabernet Sauvignon and Zinfandel.

There are at least twenty thousand names worth remembering if you're looking for well-made, good-quality wine around the world. But style and fashion are ardent masters, and a cursory glance at my cellar will show preferences for fewer than a thousand wines. Here's my very opinionated and personal list of the world's top producers.

NORTH AMERICA

UNITED STATES

Sparklers: Domaine Carneros La Rêve, Gloria Ferrar, and Roederer Estate

California

• **Chardonnay:** Anderson's Conn Valley Vineyards, Calera, Chalone Reserve, Cinnabar, Dehlinger, Paul Hobbs, Kistler, Kunde, Marcassin, Matanzas Creek, Merryvale Reserve, Neyers, Pahlmeyer, Rochioli, and Sanford Reserve

• **Gewürztraminer:** Navarro

• **Sémillon:** St. Supery

• **Sauvignon Blanc, Fumé-Blanc, and White Meritages:** Beringer, Dry Creek, Flora Springs, Honig, Kunde, Mason, Matanzas Creek, St. Supery, and Venezia

• **Other whites:** Alban, Arrowood, Bonny Doon, Murphy Goode, Andrew Murray, and Zaca Mesa

• **Cabernets, Merlots, and Meritages:** Abreu, Anderson's Conn Valley Vineyards, Araujo, Barnett, Beaulieu Vineyards, Beringer, Cain Five, Château Montelena, Château St.-Jean, Clark Claudon, Dalla Valle, Dehlinger, Dominus, Dunn, Flora Springs, Geyser Peak Block Collection and Reserves, Laurel Glen, Lokoya, Robert Mondavi Reserve, Pahlmeyer, Joseph Phelps, Pride Mountain, St. Clement, Shafer, Stag's Leap Wine Cellars, Stag's Leap Winery, and Stonestreet

• **Italian Varieties:** La Famiglia di Mondavi Barbera, Montevina Barbera, Robert Pepi Barbera, and Pietra Santa

• **Pinot Noir:** Au Bon Climat, Calera, Chalone, Dehlinger, Gary Farrell, Fiddlehead, Landmark, Lynmar, Marcassin, Rochioli, and Siduri

• **Rhône Varieties:** Alban, Au Bon Climat, Beringer, Bonny Doon, Christopher Creek, Dehlinger, Geyser Peak Reserve, Jade Mountain, Andrew Murray, Ojai, Joseph Phelps, Qupe, Ridge, Rosenblum, Swanson, Sean Thackrey, Truchard, Vigil, Wellington, and Windsor

• **Zinfandel:** Caldwell, Dashe, Edmeades, Gary Farrell, Folie à Deux, Greenwood Ridge, Hartford Court, JC Cellars, Outpost, Ravenswood, Ridge, Rosenblum, Jeff Runquist, Steele, Storybook Mountain, and Turley

• **Dessert Wines:** Château St. Jean, Kendall Jackson, Navarro, and Windsor

Oregon

Adelsheim, Bethel Heights, Brick House, Chehalem, Cristom, Domaine Drouhin, Evesham Wood, Lange, McKinlay, Shea Family, and Ken Wright

Washington State

Château Ste. Michelle, Chinook, Columbia, Dunham, Kiona, Leonetti, Matthews Cellar, Quilceda Creek, and Andrew Will

CANADA

Strong estates in British Columbia: Blue Mountain, Gehringer Brothers, Gray Monk, Mission Hill, Nichol Vineyard, Quail's Gate, Sumac Ridge, and Tinhorn Creek

Ontario

Inniskillin and Hillebrand

SOUTH AMERICA

ARGENTINA

Bodegas Norton, Bodegas Weinert, Catena, and Valentin Bianchi

CHILE

Almaviva, Casa Lapostolle, Errazuriz, Montes Alpha, Santa Rita, and Veramonte

EUROPE

AUSTRIA

Bründlmayer, Hirtzberger, Emmerich Knoll, Kracher, Nigl, Pichler, Prager, Schröck, and Umathum

FRANCE

Alsace

Beyer, Boxler, Hugel, Ostertag, Schlumberger, Trimbach, Weinbach, and Zind Humbrecht

Bordeaux

- **Bordeaux Blanc:** Carbonnieux, Domaine de Chevalier, la Garde, Haut-Brion Blanc, Larrivet Haut-Brion, Laville Haut-Brion, la Louvière, Malartic Lagravière, Olivier, Pape Clement, and Smith Haut-Lafitte

- **Margaux:** Brane Cantenac, d'Issan, Margaux, Palmer, du Tertre

- **Médoc and Haut-Médoc:** Cantemerle, Haut-Marbuzet, la Lagune, Lanessan, Potensac, and Sociando Mallet

- **Moulis and Listrac:** Poujeaux, Chasse Spleen, and Maucaillou

- **Pauillac:** Clerc Milon, Duhart Milon, Grand Puy Lacoste, Lafite-Rothschild, Latour, Lynch Bages, Mouton-Rothschild, Pichon Lalande, Pichon Baron, and Pontet Canet

- **Pessac-Léognan:** les Carmes Haut-Brion, Domaine de Chevalier, Haut-Brion, la Mission Haut-Brion, Pape Clement, Smith Haut-Lafitte, and la Tour Haut-Brion

- **Pomerol perennials:** Bon Pasteur, Certan Giraud, Certan de May, Clinet, Clos l'Eglise, la Conseillante, la Fleur de Gay, la Fleur Pétrus, la Grave à Pomerol, Latour à Pomerol, Nenin (since 1998), Trotanoy, and Vieux Château Certan

- **St.-Emilion—the stalwarts:** Ausone, l'Angelus, Beauséjour Bécot, Beauséjour Duffau, Canon, Canon la Gaffelière, Cheval Blanc, Clos Fourtet, la Dominique, Figeac, Magdelaine, Monbousquet, Pavie, le Tertre Rôteboeuf, and Troplong Mondot

- **St.-Emilion—the upstarts:** Chauvin, Clos Badon, Clos Dubreuil, Clos de l'Oratoire, Clos St.-Martin, la Couspaude, la Gomerie, Grand Mayne, Grandes Murailles, la Mondotte, Pavie Decesse, Pavie Macquin, Peby Faugères, Quinault l'Enclos, and Valandraud

- **St.-Estèphe:** Calon Segur, Cos d'Estournel, Cos Labory, Lafon Rochet, and Montrose

- **St.-Julien:** Beychevelle, Branaire, Ducru Beaucaillou, Gruaud Larose, Leoville Barton, Leoville les Cases, and Leoville Poyferre

- **Sauternes and Barsac:** Foie gras accompaniments include d'Arche, Bastor Lamontage, Broustet, Climens, Coutet, Doisy Daëne, Doisy Védrines, Gillette, Guiraud, Lafaurie Peyraguey, de Malle, Raymond Lafon, Rayne Vigneau, Rieussec, Sigalas Rabaud, Suduiraut, la Tour Blanche, and d'Yquem

- **Right bank satellites worth a drink:** Canon de Brem (Canon-Fronsac), Canon Moueix (Canon Fronsac), de Chambrun (Lalande-de-Pomerol), Dalem (Fronsac), la Dauphine (Fronsac), Grand Ormeau (Lalande-de-Pomerol), Roc de Cambes (Côtes de Bourg), and la Vieille Curée (Fronsac)

Burgundy

- **Beaujolais:** Diochon, Drouhin, Duboeuf, Pierre Ferraud, Sylvain Fessy, Jadot, Domaine de Robert, Louis Tête, Thorin, and Trenel

- **Burgundy Reds:** Comte Armand, Robert Arnoux, Billard Gonnet, Simon Bize, Jean Marc Boillot, Chandon de Briailles, Meo Camuzet, Robert Chevillon, Bruno Clair, J.J. Confuron, Domaine de Courcel, Domaine de la Romanée-Conti, Claude Dugat, Réné Engel, Vincent Girardin, Henri Gouges, Jean Grivot, A.F. Gros, Anne Gros, Michel Gros, Michel Lafarge, Dominique Laurent, Domaine Leroy, Marquis d'Angerville, Denis Mortet, Monthelie Douhairet, Georges Mugneret, Gerard Mugneret, Perrot Minot, Pousse d'Or, Daniel Rion, Emmanuel Rouget, Christian Serafin, and Comte de Vogüe

- **Burgundy Whites:** Guy Amiot, Robert Ampeau, Bonneau de Martray, Louis Carillon, Bruno Clair, Coche-Dury, Réné and Vincent Dauvissat, Joseph Drouhin, André Forest, Jean Noel Gagnard, Louis Jadot, Francois Jobard, Comte Lafon, Domaine Leflaive, Domaine Leroy, Louis Michel, Michel Neillon, Ravenneau, Ramonet, Etienne Sauzet, and Verget

Champagne

Bollinger, Deutz, Egly-Ouriet, Krug, Louis Roederer, Pol Roger, Salon, and Taittinger

Loire

• **Chinon:** Baudry, Breton, Couly-Dutheil, Druet, Joguet, and Raffault

• **Sancerre and Pouilly-Fumé:** Bourgeois, Cailbourdin, Chatelain, Cotat, Crochet, Dagueneau, Delaporte, Jolivet, Ladoucette, Mellot, and H. Reverdy

• **Savennières:** Château d'Epiré, Coulée de Serrant, Domaine Baumard, and Domaine du Closel

• **Vouvray:** Champalou, Clos Baudoin, Foreau, Gaston Huet, Vigneau-Chevreau

Rhône

• **Rhône Reds:** Beaucastel (all), Beaurenard (all), Belle Crozes-Hermitage, les Cailloux, Cayron Gigondas, Chapoutier (all), Chave, Gerard Chave-Hermitage, Clape (all), les Clefs d'Or, Clos des Papes, Jean-Luc Colombo, Courbis Cornas, Cuilleron St.-Joseph, Domaine de la Morderée, Goubert Gigondas, Graillot Crozes-Hermitage, Grippat (all), J.M. Guerin Côte-Rôtie, Guigal vineyard designated wines, Jaboulet (all), Jasmin Côte-Rôtie, Marcoux, Perret St.-Joseph, Rayas, Santa Duc Gigondas, Tardieu Laurent (all), Verset Cornas, Vieux Donjon, and Vieux Télégraphe

• **Rhône Whites:** Beaucastel (all), Chapoutier, Chave, Gerard Chave Hermitage, Domaine de la Morderée, Guigal, Jaboulet, Pichon Condrieu, Rayas (all), and Vernay Condrieu

GERMANY

Georg Breuer, von Buhl, Grünhauser, Gunderloch, Fritz Haag, Reinhold Haart, Dr. Heger, von Hövel, Toni Jost, Künstler, Dr. Loosen, Maximin, Mönchhof, Egon Müller, Müller-Catoir, Pfeffingen, J.J. Prüm, S.A. Prüm, Willi Schäfer, Dr. Thamisch, Robert Weil, Weins-Prüm, Wirsching, and Zilliken

ITALY

Abruzzi

Casal Thaulero, Illuminati, Antonio Monti, and Valentini

Basilicata

D'Angelo and Sasso

Calabria

Librandi and Nicodemo

Campania

Mastroberardino and Vadiaperti

Friuli Venezia

Abbazia di Rosazzo, Ca' Vescovo, Doro Princic, Felluga, Gradnik, Gravner, Jermann, Pecorari, Plozner, Puiatti (EnoFriuli), Radikon, Ronchi di Cialla, Ronco del Gnemiz, Russiz, Schiopetto, and La Viarte

Lazio

Falesco and Paolo di Mauro

Marches

Bucci, la Monacesca, Moroder, le Terruzzo, Umani Ronchi, and Villamagna

Molise

Di Majo Norante

Piedmont

Elio Altare, Clerico, Conterno Fontino, Einaudi, Gaja, Bruno Giacosa, Grasso, Moccagatta, Prunotto, Sandrone, Paolo Scavino, Vietti, and Roberto Voerzio

Puglia

Taurino

Sicily and the Islands

Corvo, de Bartoli, Donnafugata, Hauner, and Regaleali

Tuscany

• **Brunello di Montalcino:** Altesino, Argiano, Biondi Santi, Canalicchio di Sopra, Case Basse, Castelgiocondo, Ciacci Piccolomini d'Aragona, Col d'Orcia, Fuligni, Lisini, Pertimali, Pieve di Santa Restituta, la Poderina, Poggio Antico, Il Poggione, Scopetone, and Talenti

• **Chianti Classico:** Antinori, Badia a Coltibuono, Castallare, Castello di Ama, Castello dei Rampolla, Felsina, Fonterutoli, Fontodi, Isole e Olena, le Masse, Monsanto, Monte Vertine, Paneretta, Podere Il Palazzino, Selvapiana, and Terrabianca

• **Chianti Rufina:** Baggiolini, Capezzana, Frescobaldi, and Guicciardini Strozzi

• **Tuscan Coast:** le Macchiolo, Ornellaia, San Luigi, and Sassacaia

• **Vernaccia:** Le Colonne, San Quirico, and Terruzi & Puthod

• **Vino Nobile di Montepulciano:** Avignonesi, Bindella, Fognano, and Poliziano

Umbria

Caprai, Lungarotti, Vaselli, and Villa Antica

Veneto

Alighieri, Allegrini, Anselmi, Bertani, Gini, Lamberti, Masi, Pieropan, Quintarelli, Speri, Tomassi, and Zenato

PORTUGAL

Bright Brothers, Evel, Luis Pato, Quinta do Carmo, Quinta da Carvalhais, Quinta da Crasto, and Quinta da Pellada

• Port: Dow, Ferreira, Fonseca, Graham, Niepoort, Ramos Pinto (tawnies), Taylor, Vesuvio, and Warre

SPAIN

Abadia Retuerta, Bodegas Nekeas, Costers del Siurana, Finca Allende, Hidalgo, Lustau, Marques de Murrieta, Martin Codax, Mas Igneus, Morgadio, Muga, Pasanau, Pesquera, Remelluri, San Roman, San Vicente, Teofilo Reyes, and Vega Sicilia

AUSTRALIA AND NEW ZEALAND

AUSTRALIA

Bannockburn, Brokenwood, Cape Mentelle, Clarendon Hills, D'Arenberg, Elderton, Frankland Estate, Giaconda, Green Vineyards, Grosset, Henschke, Hewitson, Lenswood, Leeuwin Estate, Peter Lehmann, McWilliams, Mount Horrocks, Penfolds (reds) Reynella, Rosemount, St. Hallet's, Yarra Yering, and Yeringberg

NEW ZEALAND

Alpha Domus, Brancott, Cloudy Bay, Lawson's Dry Hills, Martinborough, Palliser, Sacred Hill, Allan Scott, Thornbury, Trinity Hill, and Villa Maria

SOUTH AFRICA

Backsberg, Bouchard Finlayson, Grangehurst, Kanonkop, Meerlust, Mulderbosch, Rustenberg, Thelema, Vriesenhof, and Warwick

142